MULTISKILLING:

Health Unit Coordination

FOR THE HEALTH CARE PROVIDER

ACKNOWLEDGMENTS

We wish to thank the following practitioners and educators for their critical reviews of the manuscript.

Claudeen R. Buettner, RN, EdD, College of Southern Idaho, Twin Falls, ID

Peggy L. Long, RN, BS, Lancaster General Hospital, Lancaster, PA

Claudia Manning-Weber, MS, RT(R), Adjunct Faculty, Prescott College, Prescott, AZ

Delores J. Pederson, RN, BSN, Albuquerque Technical Vocational Institute, Albuquerque, NM

Linda M. Schneider, Western Wisconsin Technical Institute, LaCrosse, WI

Julie White, RN, BSN, Wright College, Chicago, IL

Beverly M. Kovanda, PhD, Series Editor, Columbus State Community College, Columbus, OH

MULTISKILLING:

Health Unit Coordination

FOR THE HEALTH CARE PROVIDER

Rita A. Emerick,
RNC, MSN
Diana S Graham,
RNC, MSN, CS, ANP
St. Vincent Hospital, Indianapolis, IN

Beverly M. Kovanda
PhD, MS, MT, (ASCP), CLP (NCA)
Series Editor

Delmar Publishers

an International Thomson Publishing company I(T)P®

Albany • Bonn • Boston • Cincinnati • Detroit • London • Madrid
Melbourne • Mexico City • New York • Pacific Grove • Paris • San Francisco
Singapore • Tokyo • Toronto • Washington

Cover Design: Scott Keidong's Image Enterprises

Delmar Staff

Publisher: Susan Simpfenderfer
Acquisition Editor: Dawn Gerrain
Developmental Editor: Marjorie A Bruce
Project Editor: Brooke Graves/Graves Editorial Service
Team Assistant: Sandra Bruce

Production Coordinator: John Mickelbank
Marketing Manager: Darryl Caron
Marketing Coordinator: Nina Lontrato
Editorial Assistant: Donna L. Leto

COPYRIGHT © 1999
By Delmar Publishers
a division of International Thomson Publishing Inc.

The ITP logo is a trademark under license.

Printed in the United States of America

For more information, contact:
Delmar Publishers
3 Columbia Circle, Box 15015
Albany, New York 12212-5015

International Thomson Editores
Seneca 53
Colonia Polanco
11560 Mexico D. F. Mexico

International Thomson Publishing Europe
Berkshire House
168–173 High Holborn
London, WC1V7AA
United Kingdom

International Thomson Publishing GmbH
Königswinterer Strasse 418
53227 Bonn
Germany

Nelson ITP, Australia
102 Dodds Street
South Melbourne
Victoria, 3205 Australia

International Thomson Publishing Asia
60 Albert Street
#15–01 Albert Complex
Singapore 189969

Nelson Canada
1120 Birchmont Road
Scarborough, Ontario
M1K5G4, Canada

International Thomson Publishing—Japan
Hirakawa-cho Kyowa Building, 3F
2-2-1 Hirakawa-cho, Chiyoda-ku,
Tokyo 102, Japan

International Thomson Publishing France
Tour Maine-Montparnasse
33 Avenue du Maine
75755 Paris Cedex 15, France

ITE Spain/Paraninfo
Calle Magallanes, 25
28015-Madrid, Espana

1 2 3 4 5 6 7 8 9 10 XXX 03 02 01 00 99 98

Library of Congress Cataloging-in-Publication Data
Emerick, Rita A.
    Multiskilling : health unit coordination for the health care
  provider / Rita A. Emerick, Diana S. Graham
      p. cm. -- (Delmar's multiskilling series)
    Includes bibliographical references and index.
    ISBN 0-7668-0213-2
    1. Hospital ward clerks. 2. Hospital secretaries. 3. Hospitals-
-Admission and discharge. I. Title. II. Title: Health unit
coordination for the health care provider. III. Series.
      [DNLM: 1. Patient Care Management--organization & administration
programmed instruction. 2. Forms and Records Control programmed
instruction. 3. Patient Admission programmed instruction.
4. Patient Discharge programmed instruction. 5. Patient Credit and
Collection programmed instruction.   W 18.2 E54m 1999]
RA972.55.E47   1999
362.1'1'068--dc21
DNLM/DLC
for Library of Congress

98-46306
CIP

The Multiskilling for Health Care Providers series consists of the *Patient Care: Basic Skills for the Health Care Provider* core text and many separate modular texts. The Multiskilling series offers a comprehensive vision of the diversity and many implications of multiskilling, whether in an acute care setting, home care, hospice, ambulatory setting, long-term care facility, or physician's office. The core text and module subjects have been identified through research as key topics in multiskilling and patient care training across the nation.

The framework for this series is found in the historic evolution of multiskilling, the National Health Care Skill Standards, and 13 years of personal experience in developing academic materials and successfully training thousands of multiskilled health care providers in a multitude of nursing and allied health skill areas. The concept referred to as *multiskilling, cross-training*, and (more recently) *patient care skills* began to gain national awareness in the mid-1980s, as pressures for cost containment in health care intensified. Institutions began to focus on more efficient use of personnel for economic survival. The implications of managed care are far-reaching.

In 1994, the National Health Care Skill Standards were developed through a national collaborative effort of health care organizations, professional organizations, schools, and colleges of higher education. By implementing these standards, we can more effectively serve the needs of a diverse client population and maintain quality care, while increasing the efficiency of staff utilization. Health care costs can be contained; the new technology, which is changing how and where health care is delivered, can be prudently applied. We believe that the skill standards are important and so their intent has been incorporated into the entire series.

The core text, *Patient Care: Basic Skills for the Health Care Provider*, meets the OBRA requirements for basic patient care skills. These skills are required of every health care provider who undertakes client care, regardless of the institutional setting or professional affiliation.

We believe that the core-text-plus-modules concept is the only rational approach to meeting the vastly different academic and training needs in multiskilling, as we re-engineer careers in all health care settings. The modules are flexible, well written, and academically sound. The modular approach is cost-effective. A health care worker's skills can be developed based upon individual goals, institutional needs for retraining, or specific career development. Colleges, hospitals, other health care agencies, technical and career schools, and "tech prep" programs need only purchase the modules that address their unique, customized academic and training needs. Because multiskilling is market-driven, other modules continue to be developed as health care needs are identified and evolve.

The modules are written by credentialed experts in each content area and multiskilling education. They have identified essential and appropriate nursing and allied health skills that can be accurately and safety performed by nonprofessionals to enhance the quality of patient care.

The depth of theory and skills in each module goes beyond other texts, which are usually written from the perspective of one profession rather than by specialists in each identifiable allied health and nursing area. We believe that this principle provides a stronger basis for instruction and facilitates a higher level of quality patient care.

The material in each module is organized in a clear, concise, straightforward manner to make learning easier, because health care institutions are demanding shorter—but intensified—training periods. The pedagogical features enhance retention and simplify learning.

We believe that the Multiskilling series combines the knowledge, experience, successes, and expertise of all of the authors. It provides the tools and flexibility to custom-design a curriculum that truly meets worker/student professional goals, augments valuable skills, and strengthens employability, not only now but as we prepare for the 21st century.

Beverly M. Kovanda, PhD, MS, MT (ASCP), CLP (NCA)
Coordinator/Professor, Multicompetency Health Technology
Columbus State Community College, Columbus, OH

DELMAR'S MULTISKILLING SERIES

Patient Care: Basic Skills for the Health Care Provider
Multiskilling: Advanced Patient Care Skills for the Health Care Provider
Multiskilling: Phlebotomy Collection Procedures for the Health Care Provider
Multiskilling: Electrocardiography for the Health Care Provider
Multiskilling: Respiratory Care for the Health Care Provider
Multiskilling: Point of Care Testing—Capillary Puncture for the Health Care Provider
Multiskilling: Team Building for the Health Care Provider
Multiskilling: Waived Laboratory Testing for the Health Care Provider

Modules Coming Soon:
Multiskilling: Rehabilitation Services for the Health Care Provider
Multiskilling: Dietary Assisting for the Health Care Provider
Multiskilling: Radiography for the Health Care Provider

TABLE OF CONTENTS

PREFACE

Significant changes have occurred in the levels of personnel caring for patients. This module discusses the role of Health Unit Coordinator. Information contained in this module serves as a beginning reference point for the role. The individualization of this module to meet your specific needs requires you to be familiar with the legalities of your state or region, the policies and procedures in your institution, specific forms, and organizational requirements. The support of practitioners who are experienced in the areas included in this training is essential for success in your new role.

Skills included in this module may not currently be performed in health care settings in some areas of the country. We have included skills that are currently being practiced in a large midwestern hospital.

Even though we believe that anatomy and physiology, medical terminology, and coding are important components of this training, we have not covered these topics in this module. There are multiple resources in various formats (books, videos, computer-assisted instruction) available for training in these areas. The coding rules change so rapidly that it would be impossible for us to supply updates; other training support mechanisms for coding furnish such updates as they occur.

Each chapter in this module lists objectives for students, review questions, and suggested learning activities. Tables, flowcharts, and skill checklists are included to facilitate transfer of information and serve as quick references.

Because health care is always changing with new ideas, it is important that you welcome change and continue your path in lifelong learning. The likelihood that your role will constantly evolve is great.

Rita A. Emerick, RNC, MSN
Diana S. Graham, RNC, MSN, CS, ANP

Introduction to the Health Unit Coordinator Role

After reading this chapter, you will be able to:

Describe the importance of the health unit coordinator role.

List the main duties of the health unit coordinator.

Describe the relationship among the health unit coordinator, the nursing unit, and the patient.

OVERVIEW

Imagine that you have pneumonia. You're tired, are running a fever of 101, and have a painful and productive cough. Sleep deprivation has set in because you haven't slept for days. By the time you saw your primary care physician you had been sick for a week. You're dehydrated, weak, and cranky. Now, let's imagine that your physician sends you to the hospital to be admitted to a respiratory unit for some aggressive intravenous medications, fluids, and respiratory care.

You finally arrive at the hospital and find the admitting department—crowded as usual. You drag yourself to the sign-in window and tell them you are here to be admitted. The receptionist finds your name on a list and asks you to have a seat; they will be with you in "just a few moments." During the next hour, you sit next to many people with a variety of illnesses. People are coughing to your right and left, and then there's that strange young man with the odd-colored rash all over what you can see of his body. Finally, your name is called and you gather up your hastily packed bag and go to a stuffy cubicle located just off the main thoroughfare of the hospital. Here you are asked what seems like a million questions—your age, if you work, where and how long you have worked, insurance coverage—the list of questions seems endless. Finally the interrogation ends, and the clerk tells you to go back to your seat in the waiting room and someone will be with you "in just a few moments" to take you to your room. CAN'T SOMEONE SEE I AM SICK AND NEED TO LIE DOWN? You want to shout this, but instead you take your seat and wait . . . and wait . . . and *wait*.

Please tell me there's another way to handle this! Let's imagine a different scenario, and you decide which patient you would want to be. You are still the cranky, tired, feverish person described earlier. However, the hospital where you are sent for admission has unit health unit coordinators who do the unit-based admission procedures. Upon arrival, you are taken directly to your respiratory unit and greeted by that unit's staff. They see how uncomfortable you are and one of the nurses takes you *to your own room*, where you can lie down, get a little oxygen, and rest. Here, the health unit coordinator asks you the same questions and wants to see the same insurance cards, but you are in your own room, lying in a bed, not surrounded by other people with various ailments and prying eyes. After getting all the necessary information, the health unit coordinator leaves you in the care of your nurses, who can start the treatments your physician intended.

Which patient would you rather be? Today's health care consumers are demanding better care. They are unhappy with long waits for admission procedures and having to repeat the same personal data to several different people. They are impatient with a general lack of communication from one caregiver to another. Patients are being cared for by many different professions. All of these care providers are looking for easy access to patients, charts, test results, and other information. Nurses are dissatisfied with having no voice in the placement of clients on the unit, physicians are confused about where to find their patients, and finance departments need huge amounts of information to provide appropriate coverage. The admitting scenario described is just one of the many functions of the health unit coordinator—but what a different impression this makes on patients! It will be a big factor when they choose which health care facility they would rather go to.

CHARACTERISTICS OF THE ROLE

Your role of health unit coordinator is vital to the smooth functioning of the unit. You will probably be the first person patients come into contact with when they come to your facility or when you call them concerning a planned admission. Your concern, confidence, and professional ability will either make them feel at ease or make them wonder just what type of facility they are entrusting their health care to. Professional abilities are gauged by clients in many different ways. When patients first come to your unit, they notice your facial expressions, tone of voice, grooming, and professional appearance. In person or on the telephone, they notice when you appear truly interested in taking care of their needs.

COMPONENTS OF THE ROLE

There are many components in the complex role of the health unit coordinator: reception, preadmission work, admission procedures, **financial coordination**, medical records processing, and basic secretarial responsibilities for the unit. In this section we look at what services and functions can be done, by this one position, that would enhance the function of a unit.

Reception

Ask any large business the importance of the receptionist and you will be told the overwhelming value of this position. You will be that first contact, that first impression for your facility. Many times your actual workstation will be near the entrance to the unit. This area will become the unit's nerve center, with nurses discussing the admissions and discharges, physicians looking for their patients, other departments looking for patients to transport to testing and treatment areas, insurance companies looking for **verification** of admissions and discharges, and constant telephone calls with information to be processed. In the midst of this chaos you will also be the one visitors go to for information and guidance, mail and flower distribution, and anything and everything else.

Preadmission Work

Initial contact with the patients may occur before they arrive at your facility or hospital. Many times the physician will call ahead and notify your unit of a scheduled admission for that day or some time in the future. After you receive basic information, such as the patient's name, diagnosis, and telephone number, you may then make the initial contact with the patient. Depending on your facility, you may need unique items of information that are easier to obtain before the patient arrives. Some standards of information are listed in Table 1–1. After all the necessary information has been obtained, you will need

■ **financial coordination:** *arrangement of methods to allow payment for services provided by the facility; includes working closely with insurance carriers, government programs, and personal payment programs*

■ **verification:** *contacting the insurance company or government agency that will be responsible for the financial reimbursement to the hospital for services provided to the patient*

Table 1-1 Preadmission Information

1. Patient's full name	Include middle and maiden names.
2. Patient's full address	Include zip code and county of residence. Don't forget box numbers, full street names, and route numbers.
3. Employer's name, address, and telephone number	Complete this as much as possible. It is also important to get the spouse's employer information as well, in case they have insurance coverage from both employers.
4. Insurance carrier	Include name, address, telephone numbers, and any special notification requirements of the company. This information is usually located on the patient's identification card. This is also a good time to be alert for any special financial circumstances, such as no insurance, **Medicaid**, or multiple insurance carriers.
5. Emergency information	Get names, addresses, telephone numbers, and relationship(s) to patient.
6. Special information for discharge	This is a good time to note patients who may need extra discharge assistance. Be alert to clients who come from **extended care facilities** or retirement homes; elderly patients who live alone or who are sole caregivers to spouses or children; patients with disabilities such as speech or hearing impairments; and patients who have difficulties with ambulation or with independent self-care.

■ **Medicaid:** *a federal health insurance plan, authorized by Title XIX of the Social Security Act (Public Law No. 89-97); administered by individual states to provide health care for the poor*

■ **extended care facilities:** *usually refers to some type of nursing home or transitional care establishment*

to generate and assemble the patient's chart (this is discussed further in Chapter 3). This chart may be kept in your own area or taken to another designated location in your facility.

Admission

When patients arrive for admission to your unit, they will be nervous, cautious, and often in pain or discomfort. Your first priority is to provide for their immediate needs. If the patient tells you of pain or discomfort, seek assistance from the nurses on your unit. Let them decide whether the patient can remain in the admitting area to answer your questions, or if they need to take the patient to a room immediately to provide care. If the patient and nurses tell you it is suitable for the patient to answer questions in your area, provide comfortable seating and devote your attention to that patient. Do not neglect the spouse or person who has accompanied the patient to your facility. First, ask the patient if he or she prefers that person to stay or to wait elsewhere. It is always the patient's decision as to who is entitled to hear confidential information. If you were alerted earlier to this patient's arrival, you may already have had many of the questions answered, and need only to verify information. If not, remember that patients do get tired of answering the same questions over and over. Listen closely and try to get the needed information as quickly as possible. Refer to Table 1-2 for sample questions.

Copy both sides of all insurance cards or verifications. Most information regarding insurance filing can be found directly on the cards. Ask patients if they wish any restrictions, such as advance directives (discussed in Chapter 3) or directions that no information is to be given out regarding their hospitalization.

When you have completed all necessary forms and have the patient's signature on any consents for treatments and insurance releases for information, make sure the patients get to their rooms as soon as possible. That may mean

Table 1-2 Sample Questions

Question	Significance
1. Full name and address	Important for patient identification, billing, and chart maintenance.
2. Reason for admission	Clarification of expectations for hospitalization.
3. Social Security number	Patient identification.
4. Emergency notification	Identification of who to contact if patient's condition changes.
5. Name, address, and telephone number of employer and spouse's employer	May have to be contacted concerning benefits.
6. Full insurance information; including all insurance coverages	Many people are covered by more than one insurance company; needed to verify coverage.
7. Physician's name	Some patients will have more than one physician who must be notified of the admission.

that you or one of the other members of the health care team takes them to the room. Whoever escorts patients to their rooms is responsible for leaving them in a safe environment, either sitting in a chair or lying in the bed. NEVER leave a confused patient alone in a new room. If your patient appears confused or in discomfort, stay with him or her until a nurse or another member of the clinical team takes over.

Order Transcription

In some facilities the health unit coordinator is responsible for transcribing physician and other health care professionals' orders. In other institutions, the actual health care provider does this. Check with your individual institution to determine whose job this is. Basically, order transcription involves the processing of the written order into action. For example: a physician writes an order for a lab study in the patient's medical record. Order transcription is the process by which this is made to happen.

There are various methods of order transcription throughout the health care industry. Some examples of guidelines for processing are:

1. Computerized order entry. In some institutions the health care provider enters an order into a computer. Orders are sent automatically through the system to, for example, a lab phlebotomist, who comes to the patient, draws blood, transports the sample back to the lab for processing, and enters the results in the computer system for the health care team to review.
2. Secretarial order entry. Someone—frequently the health unit coordinator—is responsible for reviewing the orders, sending the proper requisitions to the appropriate areas, and ensuring that the work is completed.
3. Patient-focused teams. In some institutions each member of the care team is responsible for processing the orders on the team's own patients. The team members review the order and complete the task if appropriate, or communicate with the people who will be doing the task, to coordinate the order with the patient's plan of care. To continue the lab example, the physician would write the order, and then the caregiver could draw the blood immediately and start the processing faster, with fewer personnel,

and without any duplication of effort. Or, the health care provider could review the appropriateness of the order and discuss the situation with the physician immediately, before completing the order process.

Financial Arrangements

Taking care of the financial arrangements for the patient's care is a very important part of your role. You will need to verify the insurance carrier as soon as possible, either before the patient arrives at the hospital or after the admission. Many companies make it the responsibility of the patient to call the company before going to the facility. Whether or not the patient has called, you will need to contact the insurance company to verify and ensure coverage. Many insurance carriers have **case managers** who follow each patient's progress through the hospitalization. You may be the person who will continue to notify the case manager of the patient's condition, or you may turn this task over to a utilization review or case manager within your own facility. If you will be the one who updates the insurance company's case manager, make sure you get that person's name and document all pertinent information for each conversation. See Chapter 5 for further discussion of financial verification and counseling.

■ *case manager:* a designated person responsible for coordinating the care of the patient. May be employed by the facility or the insurance company that is responsible for payment. Responsibilities include matching appropriate levels of care with patient conditions

Medical Records Handling

Medical records are usually complex and confusing. Proper handling of the record allows all members of the health care team to document the care given and to see easily and quickly what care was given by others. Your responsibilities for the medical record include assembling the initial chart, replacing chart forms as needed by the caregivers, and posting lab data and reports within the record. In some facilities you may be required to do concurrent analysis (discussed in Chapter 3). Keep in mind that the medical record is always a legal record and may be used later, even in a court of law, if any questions arise concerning patient care or treatment. Because it is a legal record, it must be maintained in an orderly and confidential manner at all times.

Upon discharge of a patient, you will be required to assemble all portions of the record and ensure that the record is complete before it is sent for storage. This will mean looking at all aspects of the chart for proper signatures and documentation. There will be some method for you to mark charts where signatures are needed by physicians and nurses, and it will be your responsibility to ensure that they are completed. Refer to Chapter 6 for further information on care of the patient's chart at discharge.

Basic Secretarial Functions

You are the secretary of the unit. This means it is your responsibility to re-order and stock all chart- and office-related supplies. You will be the one person who communicates bed assignments to all other departments within the facility. This includes the receipt and delivery of pertinent information to central facility departments. You will coordinate schedules for testing and transportation for your clients throughout their stays. You will be responsible for maintaining all files that pertain to the unit and your clients.

In summary, the health unit coordinator must be well-organized, friendly, patient, well-mannered, well-groomed, and well-informed, and must be able to perform many functions at once without appearing hurried or harried. The abilities of this person, and the impressions he or she makes on all patients, departments, and health care providers, strengthen or hinder the unit tremendously.

▰▰▰▰ SAMPLE JOB DESCRIPTION

The job description of the health unit coordinator will vary from facility to facility. A sample job description is shown in Figure 1–1. Make sure that you read your own job description thoroughly and ask any questions regarding the expectations when you start your new role. Many sections of the job description will vary from facility to facility, for everything from what the major functions of the role are to who your immediate supervisor is. For example, most likely the health unit coordinator will report to a unit supervisor, director, or manager; however, in many team-based practices this person reports to the entire health care team. You will probably find many variations to this role as it is modified to meet the demands of your facility.

I. POSITION TITLE: Health Unit Coordinator

II. DEPARTMENT AND SECTION: ABC

III. POSITION SUMMARY:
This position supports the work of the Operating Unit by performing various business office and related patient functions. Assigned tasks include, but are not limited to: admitting, discharge screening, medical recording coding and abstracting, insurance verification and certification, reception, and coordination of financial arrangements. The incumbents act as representatives of the unit and demonstrate the XYZ philosophy of caring in all aspects of job performance.

IV. MAJOR JOB FUNCTIONS:

   A. Admissions/Preadmissions

      1. Obtains biographical, financial, and insurance information from the patient or family to complete preadmission or admission process. Enters information into computer system.

      2. Verifies and monitors insurance; obtains precertifications and certifications from insurance companies. Monitors approximate hospital bill and coordinates financial arrangements with clients or family, when necessary.

   B. Medical Record Handling

      1. Performs concurrent analysis and communicates deficiencies to the appropriate persons. Works with care teams to keep charts current and complete.

      2. Distributes lab results, transcriptions, etc. to care team for review and placement in chart.

      3. Restocks chart forms.

      4. Assembles and codes charts.

      5. Collaborates with physician to obtain attestation upon discharge.

      6. Abstracts quality review data as specified by central departments.

   C. Communication and Reception

      1. Provides reception functions for visitors, patients, and physicians.

      2. Answers telephone and coordinates communication between departments and unit associates.

   D. Patient and Unit Support

      1. Generates and maintains census lists and other ad hoc reports reflecting patient data.

      2. Manages radiology films and EKG strips.

      3. Schedules procedures with ancillary departments, as needed.

      4. Orders and maintains administrative supplies.

Figure 1–1 XYZ Facility Job Description

continues

        5. Performs runner functions, including delivery of charts, radiology films, and EKGs.

    E. Support of Unit-Based Activities (some activities may be specific to unit patient population)

        1. Ensures and promotes a clean and safe environment.

        2. Attends in-services and unit meetings, and contributes to unit problem-solving activities.

        3. Actively participates in unit quality assurance activities.

        4. Performs all other duties as requested.

V. QUALIFICATIONS:

    A. Education (classroom): High school diploma required. Must achieve 9th grade math and 11th grade reading comprehension. Knowledge of medical terminology required. Additional training in customer relations and/or medical recording coding is desirable.

    B. Experience (on the job): At least two years of experience in a health care environment. Experience in one of the following areas is desirable: certification, coordination of financial arrangements, admitting, medical record coding/abstracting. Experience in computerized recordkeeping is essential. Some experience in dealing with the general public is required.

    C. Special Training, Licensure, or Credentialing: Must successfully complete medical terminology screening.

    D. Personal Skills, Aptitudes, and Qualities (includes requirements for and nature of confidentiality): Must display the ability to preserve patient dignity, privacy, and confidentiality. Must be able to communicate effectively with patients, families, medical teams, insurance companies, and other unit staff. Patience, tact, organizational skills, and flexibility are essential. Must be able to set priorities for work based on the activity of the operating unit.

    E. Work Environment and Schedule: Ability to be flexible in work schedule and job assignments is essential.

VI. CONTACTS:

    A. Internal: Various departments and associates.

    B. External: Clients, families, visitors, insurance companies, physicians, and suppliers.

VII. ORGANIZATIONAL RELATIONSHIPS:

    A. Reports to: Clinical manager.

    B. Supervises (directly): Not applicable.

    C. Committee Responsibilities: Applicable unit-based activities.

VIII. PHYSICAL REQUIREMENTS:

    A. Good vision and hearing.

    B. Minimal lifting (less than 20 lbs.).

    C. Walk unassisted without difficulty.

Written by: _____ Date: _____

Approved by: _____ Date: _____

Audited by: _____ Date: _____

8 CHAPTER 1

REVIEW QUESTIONS

Multiple Choice Questions

1. The first person the patient usually sees when coming into your facility is the:
   a. health unit coordinator.
   b. physician.
   c. nurse.
   d. clinical manager.

2. Which of the following clients is more likely to have additional discharge planning needs?
   a. A 23-year-old college student coming in for an appendectomy
   b. A 75-year-old man who lives alone coming in for a possible stroke
   c. A married 45-year-old female coming in for a scheduled hysterectomy
   d. A 5-year-old patient coming in for a tonsillectomy

3. Where is the telephone number of the insurance company most often found?
   a. In a special insurance policy
   b. In the telephone book
   c. On the back of the insurance card
   d. The patient should have this number memorized

4. If your patient is in pain or discomfort upon admission, which of the following actions should you take?
   a. Talk slowly to get all the information you will need
   b. Notify a unit nurse to evaluate the patient
   c. Call the patient's physician for the needed information
   d. Take the patient's blood pressure and pulse to evaluate his or her status, before attempting to obtain the necessary information

5. Which of the following are responsibilities of the health unit coordinator?
   a. Reception
   b. Admission procedures
   c. Medical record maintenance
   d. All of these

6. Because you are usually the first person a patient sees who represents the hospital, it is important for you to consider your:
   a. tone of voice.
   b. facial expressions.
   c. personal appearance.
   d. all of these.

7. A medical record is considered complete when:
   a. lab results are posted.
   b. physician and nursing signatures are obtained.
   c. the chart is assembled according to medical records protocol.
   d. all of these.

8. What document informs you of your job responsibilities?
   a. Policy and procedure manual
   b. Job description
   c. Hospital regulations
   d. Unit or department roles

SUGGESTED LEARNING ACTIVITIES

1. Review several job descriptions from various local health care facilities for the health unit coordinator. Compare and contrast job responsibilities, job tasks, and reporting structures.

2. Review differences between job responsibilities within your own institution for the health unit coordinator, the registered nurse, the licensed practical nurse, and the unlicensed assistive personnel.

3. Discuss how all members of the health care team rely on each other to ensure the best possible patient care and continuity.

Communication Techniques

After reading this chapter, you will be able to:

Define and give examples of confidential information.

Discuss the importance of maintaining confidentiality.

Describe "blocks" to good communication.

Identify verbal and nonverbal communication differences.

Illustrate examples of good communication techniques.

Demonstrate good telephone communication skills.

Provide examples of good written communication styles.

■ **confidentiality:**
protecting information given from or observed by one person to another

OVERVIEW

In today's world of easy access into all areas of our lives, **confidentiality** can be a difficult principle to uphold. In the health care setting, maintaining confidentiality refers to safeguarding any information given by the patient to any member of the health care team. The understanding is that this information, either written or verbal, is to be used only for the care and treatment of the patient's problems. Any other use of this information constitutes a **breach** in trust and ethics.

■ **breach:** *break*

> *Whatever in connection with my professional practice, or not in connection with it, I see or hear, in the life of men, which ought not be spoken abroad, I will not divulge, as reckoning that all should be kept secret.*
>
> —FROM THE HIPPOCRATIC OATH

Even though Hippocrates wrote these words centuries ago, they still apply today. All physicians and health care team members are bound by these words. It is the responsibility of each individual staff member to evaluate the work environment, processes, and systems for situations in which sensitive and/or confidential information is not adequately protected.

CONFIDENTIALITY

■ **privileged information:**
information that is obtained due to position or responsibilities

Just what is confidential and **privileged information**? You will be surrounded by information regarding patients on a daily basis. This may make it hard to distinguish what is and what is not confidential information. Examples of confidential information include:

1. Any information given verbally by a patient.
2. Any information the physician or health care team member obtains during an examination or in providing care.
3. Any information gained from a third person during treatment.
4. Any medical or diagnostic data that may be gathered.

The medical record is full of confidential information. Who "owns" this medical record? The original medical record is the property of the hospital or facility and should not be removed unless required by a court of law. As property of the hospital or facility, the medical record may be used by the facility for any legitimate business purpose, without specific written authorization by the patient. Proper uses include: provision of patient care, securing of payment from third parties, collection of accounts, litigation defense, quality assurance/risk management, peer review, scientific research, statistical analysis, and assistance in providing education.

The patient does have the right to his or her own records and should be accommodated according to the policies and procedures of your facility. Most facilities require notification to the physician regarding the patient's request to view or copy any part of the medical record. This notification is usually done so the physician can discuss any sections of the record with the patient that the patient may not understand fully. Seldom are these requests refused except when the patient making the request is incompetent. Discharged patients usually have no difficulty obtaining a copy of their records if they sign a release agreement. Refer to your own facility's policy and procedures for releasing patient records.

Faxing of patient information presents another confidentiality dilemma. Information regarding the patient is usually faxed only to provide emergency information needed for the direct care and treatment of the individual. There is no sure way to ensure the confidentiality of faxed materials and thus faxes should be used cautiously. Many facilities use a call-ahead and call-back system to ensure that the correct party has received the faxed materials. Verify the faxing policies in your own facility to maintain confidentiality standards.

What constitutes nonconfidential information? Name, address, sex, marital status, and other such general data are usually not considered confidential pieces of information, because they can be obtained by several means. However, they should be shared with others only in the context of providing patient care. Be alert to situations in which the patient has stated that *no* information may be given out to visitors or anyone else. These situations are usually addressed in your institution's policies, which set up some method of marking the patient's records. In normal situations, when a coworker asks you if a mutual acquaintance is a patient, does it constitute a breach in confidentiality to tell him or her? If your coworker has no need to know for the provision of care for this particular patient, then yes, it is a breach. You need to help each other stay focused on the patient's right to privacy.

You decide if confidentiality has been breached in the following cases:
1. Mary is caring for a new patient on her unit and learns that the patient's niece is her daughter's best friend. When she gets home, she tells her daughter that her friend's aunt is ill.
2. Going to work in the morning, you pass the information desk and overhear a visitor asking about the whereabouts of a patient on your unit. You, being the friendly person you are, stop and offer to take the visitor to your unit.
3. You are in the cafeteria and your friend asks you about her neighbor, who was admitted on your unit. You tell her that her neighbor will be having some tests today and that she had a bad night.
4. You had a very upsetting day and your significant other takes you to dinner. You tell your partner about a very rude patient and family.

All of these examples demonstrate a breach in confidentiality!

PERSONAL COMMUNICATION

■ *personal communication:* conversation with another person, one-to-one

What is **personal communication**? It seems so easy. You just tell people what they want to know or ask them what you need to know. Ah, if only it were that simple! How we communicate with others makes the difference in finding out the right information or creating roadblocks to information transfer. How you ask a question or give instructions is just as important as what you say. It has been said that it costs six times more to attract a new customer than it takes to

■ *customer satisfaction:*
when person receiving service
is contented with amount or
type of service rendered

keep an old one and that a typical dissatisfied customer will tell nine to eleven people about his or her problems. **Customer satisfaction** spells success and customer dissatisfaction spells failure. Customers equate good communication with good service.

Good Communication Techniques

Some tips on good communication techniques include the following:
1. Connect with those you serve.
   - Smile
   - Make eye contact
   - Introduce yourself
   - Ask the patient his or her name
   - Call people by their names
2. Treat others as you would like to be treated or as you would like your family members to be treated.
   - Do not judge
   - Be accepting
   - Offer respect
3. Look for opportunities to be courteous.
   - Open doors
   - Offer directions
   - Say "please" and "thank you"
4. Explain what you are doing. Waiting patients deserve to know why they are waiting.
5. Respect the privacy of others.
   - Knock when you enter rooms
   - Maintain confidentiality when discussing privileged information
   - Draw the privacy curtain around the bed if the room is shared with another patient
6. Provide a calm environment.
   - Keep the volume and tone of your voice at a conversation level
   - Open and close doors and drawers quietly
7. Talk on the telephone in the same manner as you would if the patient were standing in front of you.
   - Smile when you talk
   - Listen attentively to the caller
   - Do not put callers on hold without asking and obtaining their permission
   - Remain calm if the caller is agitated
8. Greet your patients with a smile and enthusiasm that makes them glad you were the one available to help them with their needs.

Barriers to Communication

Common barriers to good communication include the following:
1. *Being apathetic.* If you don't care about a situation or problem, you probably won't care whether it is resolved correctly.
2. *Refusing responsibility for problem solving.* Each of us can probably describe a situation in which we have asked for help and been told that a problem is "not in my job description" or "not my station."
3. *Being "too busy."* Sometimes people can spend extraordinary amounts of time just telling you how busy they are. We do find time to do the things that are important to us. Granted, many times one task will outweigh another in priority, but a simple explanation or referral to another resource doesn't take that much time.
4. *Using a patronizing or condescending manner.* Observing the old rule about treating others as you would like to be treated speaks volumes about your communication skills. Many of the people you will be dealing with will be under overwhelming stress or in personal pain, but this does not usually

make them mentally incompetent. Address no one as "honey," "sweetie," "grandma," or any other such name unless expressly invited to do so by that person. All patients deserve our respect and attention.

5. *Giving the "runaround."* It usually takes just as much time and effort to tell people the right information as it does to give them the wrong information. Actually, when you give them wrong or misguided information, it usually requires more of your time when they come back to you frustrated and angry.

No one likes being presented with barriers, and each of us deals with them in a different manner. Some people withdraw and silently vow never to approach you for help again. Some people agree with you just to shut you up. Some people respond with aggressive behavior. Dealing with these people takes extra time and effort. A smaller percentage of people try constructive techniques to enhance the communication.

WORKING WITH DIFFICULT PATIENTS

Emotions sometimes make us behave in ways we do not intend. The nicest, most well-mannered person in the world can become aggressive, hostile, and threatening when faced with special circumstances. Most of the people you will be dealing with will either be in pain, worried about their health, anxious about an upcoming procedure or surgery, or worried about a loved one. If you can pull back mentally and take a good look at the person who is verbally abusing you, what do you see? Is the person scared, frightened, or in pain? Is she frustrated from getting the runaround because of another person's poor communication style? Is he suffering from some medical condition that has altered his mental status? Put yourself in the patients' position for one moment. This will not change the situation. They may still be in pain. They may still be confused. But it may change the way you respond to them.

Communication Techniques

There are many techniques to use when working with difficult patients and people.

- Choose to respond, not to react. Good communication abilities allow you to put your feelings aside and address the content of the communication, not the style. We cannot control how the patient communicates, but we can control how we will respond.

- Depersonalize the situation. Try to remember that patients do not know you. They are responding to a particular problem or situation. Don't take it personally.

- Provide assurance. Remember that your patient may be in a very unfamiliar situation. Do everything in your power to resolve the complaint, whether you do it or get someone else to do it. Ask patients what resolution they desire.

- Write it down. Take notes during your discussion and be as specific as possible. What was the original conflict? What has been done? What does the patient expect to happen? Let the patient see that you are interested in getting to the facts of the matter.

- Allow the patient to vent. Sometimes people just need to work through their frustrations with the situation. After they have been allowed to express themselves, without being judged, you can reflect on what the true problem is. A reflective comment such as "Now, if I understand you correctly, the problem is . . ." This allows the patient either to correct you if you have misunderstood or to validate your understanding.

- End the discussion. If at any time you feel that you are in physical danger, stop the conversation. Tell the patient that you are uncomfortable with the

■ **mediator:** *uninvolved third party who may intervene to settle a dispute*

situation and call on an outside **mediator** or security personnel. Whether or not the threat is real, you will not be at your best if you are afraid.

■ Follow up. You will be judged, either fairly or unfairly, by how you follow up on a situation. If everything goes well, a follow-up call will show your concern for the patient's welfare. If resolution has not been reached, find out why and ask what you can do to help the process.

▓▓▓ VERBAL AND NONVERBAL COMMUNICATION TECHNIQUES

Communication occurs on a variety of levels. Verbal communication is commonly considered the only source of real information. How we interpret this verbal data, however, is based as much on *how* something is said as to *what* was actually said. How often have you been put off by salespersons who answer your questions but are gruff, frowning, or doing other things while they talk to you? The information may be correct, but your response is not the same as if they looked at you, smiled, and made you feel that you were an important part of their job.

Be aware of other things you do, without the intention of demeaning, that may be interpreted as such. Things like chewing gum, processing paperwork, and reading the computer screen all make the customers feel like they are interrupting your real work, and that they are not as important to you.

▓▓▓ TELEPHONE COMMUNICATION

■ **etiquette:** *manners; method of responding to or treating other individuals*

Telephone communication has its own unique rules for good **etiquette** in today's customer service world. Follow these simple rules to develop good telephone manners.

1. Answer the telephone promptly. If you are engaged in a conversation in person, excuse yourself and answer the telephone. Be careful not to make the person you were talking with feel dismissed. This may mean that you must ask callers if you can call them back, if you can put them on hold, or if you can take a message.
2. Identify yourself properly and clearly. "Good morning. This is Susie Smith, health unit coordinator for XYZ. How may I help you?"
3. Speak clearly into the telephone. Hold the telephone so that you speak directly into the mouthpiece. Clamping the telephone with your shoulder or with your head turned away will only muffle your voice and exasperate the caller. Let the tone of your voice smile to the customer. Never talk on the telephone while eating, chewing gum, or drinking anything.
4. Give the caller your attention. Keep a notepad and pencil by the telephone and make it a habit to take notes.
5. Write down the caller's name and use it in your conversation. Write down any dates or figures mentioned in the conversation and repeat them back to the caller. This reinforces callers' confidence that you understand their concerns and verifies that you have written the information accurately.
6. Obtain complete information. If you are taking a message, make sure you know the following:
   ■ Who the message is for
   ■ The name of the caller
   ■ The time of the call
   ■ The purpose of the call
   ■ Whether a return call is expected. (If so, get the number and a preferred time, if necessary, or note any limits on the time the caller will be available.)
7. Never leave the patient without direction. If there is a question that you cannot resolve or an answer that you do not know, do not say "I don't know." Instead, tell the patient that you will find out, or refer patients to

the correct source and then transfer them yourself. When transferring a call, give the patient the number to call if he or she is accidentally cut off. Figure 2–1 shows an example of an evaluation tool for monitoring good communication skills.

Name		Date		
Interaction	Standard	Rating: 1 = Unacceptable 2 = Meets standard 3 = Exceeds standard	Initials	Comments
Acknowledging patient	Greets patient (by name if known) with a smile within 30 seconds of patient's arrival at work station.			
Answering telephone	Answers telephone within three sets of rings, with a smile, using facility name, department name, and first name. Example: "XYZ facility, ABC department. This is Susie. How may I help you?" or "How may I direct your call?"			
Placing caller on hold	If a call must be placed on hold, asks the caller's permission and waits for a response before doing so. "May I place you on hold, please?" NOT "Hold, please."			
Excusing oneself from a customer to answer the telephone.	Excuses self from the person with whom student is conversing before answering the telephone by saying, "Please excuse me while I answer this call."			
Excusing oneself from the telephone to answer a patient.	Excuses self from the telephone call to acknowledge the person before student by saying: "Good morning (afternoon). I will be with you as soon as I finish this call."			
Transferring a call	First, gives the caller the name and telephone number of the department to which the caller is being transferred, then asks the caller to hold while student completes the transfer. Example: "ABC department number is 555-5555. Will you please hold while I connect you? Thank you."			

Figure 2–1   Health unit coordinator standards for customer interactions

▧▧▧ WRITTEN COMMUNICATION TECHNIQUES

You may be asked to write memos or letters of inquiry to many other departments, companies, facilities, individuals, or physicians. How you present yourself in your writing style may be the only image the receiver has of you and your facility. Use the following guidelines in your written communications.

1. First, always be gracious. Even if you are writing to complain about a service, your goal is to have the person continue to read what you have taken the time to write. Address the recipient by name if known. Begin the letter or communication on a positive note. For example, "I was happy to have had the opportunity to meet with you" or "We have enjoyed doing business with your company for the past few years." Try to establish a good relationship early in the correspondence.

2. Be professional. Address people by their titles unless otherwise instructed. Mr., Mrs., Ms., or Dr. should be used whenever possible. Take the effort to find out their titles or credentials before sending the correspondence.

3. Be concise. Recipients' time is just as important as your time. State the reason for your letter within the first paragraph. State what outcomes you expect to have happen and your actions. Try to make all correspondence one page if possible.

4. Be considerate. If you want people to call you back, give them the number and times you will be available for their calls. If you want them to contact someone else, give them the names and numbers they will need.

Remember, the best way to get a response from your correspondence is to give the person the tools or information needed to respond.

▧▧▧ COMMUNICATION AT WORK

Techniques for good communication apply to coworkers as well as clients. It is easy to slide by and forget good communication skills when we talk to our peers, our supervisors, and others we see on a daily basis. The health care area is constantly changing and all members of the team are under tremendous amounts of stress on a daily basis. Practicing good communication skills and techniques with each other will not only enhance your working relationship, but also, it is hoped, will make these skills second nature to you. You will not have to consciously think of what to do when a difficult situation arises, because good communication is now your way of life.

REVIEW QUESTIONS

Multiple Choice Questions

1. Confidentiality is the responsibility of which of the following?
   a. Patient
   b. Physician
   c. Nurses
   d. Each individual

2. Which of the following is not technically considered normal confidential information?
   a. Patient's name
   b. Patient diagnosis
   c. Results of any tests
   d. Prognosis

3. A patient wants to read his chart. Which of the following do you do?
   a. Copy the chart for him to read after discharge
   b. Tell him that it is against the law
   c. Follow the policy and procedure of your facility
   d. Ask him to sign a release of confidentiality

4. Good communication techniques include:
   a. smiling when talking, either in person or on the telephone.
   b. making eye contact.
   c. respecting the privacy of others.
   d. all of these.

5. Which of the following is a barrier to good communication?
   a. Apathy
   b. Refusing responsibility
   c. Patronizing behavior
   d. All of these

6. If a patient is being verbally abusive to you, what steps should you take?
   a. Run away
   b. Respond to the patient in the same communication style they are using
   c. Tell them that you are uncomfortable and call for a mediator or security personnel
   d. Threaten the patient with legal action

7. Why are "difficult" patients difficult?
   a. They may be in pain
   b. They may be angry
   c. They may be afraid or frustrated
   d. All of these

8. Taking notes when talking with a patient does which of the following?
   a. Reinforces the patient's confidence that you are interested and understand his or her concerns

   b. Threatens the patient that you are planning legal action against him or her
   c. Makes the patient think that you are not listening
   d. All of these

9. The hospital may use the medical record for all of the following except:
   a. risk management.
   b. news releases.
   c. litigation defense.
   d. scientific research.

10. If a patient requests that no information be given out to visitors, this means:
    a. you need to follow the hospital policy.
    b. you can give information to the family only.
    c. the hospital operator can give the room number only.
    d. the news media is asked to not publish the admission.

SUGGESTED LEARNING ACTIVITIES

1. Discuss various situations in which students have felt that their own confidentiality was breached.

2. Role-play situations illustrating both good and bad communication techniques.

3. Monitor controlled telephone situations. Provide feedback regarding good and bad telephone communication techniques.

The Medical Record

After reading this chapter, you will be able to:

Assemble a medical record.

Process a patient's medical chart.

Develop a working relationship with a medical records resource.

Provide concurrent analysis of a medical record.

Identify and describe the importance of advance directives.

OVERVIEW

Maintenance of the patient's medical record (chart) is a vital component of any patient's total health care. This record provides information to all health care team members. It will be used by physicians searching for vital laboratory and clinical data. It will be used by consulting physicians, therapists, and health care providers who need to know more about the patient's history prior to their involvement. The medical record will follow the patient forever, keeping track of what happened, when, and why. It will be consulted by payers who want to know what was done and why they should pay for it. It will be consulted by financial departments to decide what and how to bill. Most importantly, this is a legal record—remember this and treat it as such.

ASSEMBLY OF THE MEDICAL RECORD (CHART)

The task of assembling a patient's chart is very specific to the policies and procedures of your institution, but we will address some examples and commonalties you will most likely encounter. Medical records must be assembled in the same manner for all patients, to make referencing the chart easy for all disciplines. This process may be done twice for each patient: once at the patient's admission and again after the patient has been discharged from your facility. The following is an example of the process for assembly of an admission packet.

1. *Preadmission call to the patient for initial information or the admission interview.* On scheduled admissions (admits), the health unit coordinator can contact patients before admission to discuss the admission process. This contact should cover the following information, making the admission process easier and giving an opportunity to determine any special needs of the patients prior to admission:

   a. *Reason for hospitalization.* Why are these patients coming to your hospital? What do they expect? What have their physicians told them would be done?

   b. *Physician.* Ask about all the physicians the patients think might be involved in their care. Often the admitting physician is a surgeon or other specialist and not the primary care physician. You will need to identify all the physicians you can so that you can notify them when the patient arrives.

c. *Expectations related to the admission process.* Have these patients ever been to your hospital before? Do they know where to come? Where to park? What time they will be arriving? Who will be coming with them? What questions do they have for you regarding this process?

d. *Insurance coverage.* Remind the patients what cards or forms they need to bring with them to the hospital on the day of admission. Some insurance companies or managed care providers require that patients call the company before going into the hospital. Help the patients understand these directions, which are usually printed directly on the insurance card. Be sure to ask for all insurance coverage. Many people have primary, secondary, and even third-level insurance coverage. If you don't know, and if you don't call the insurance carriers, many times they will not pay.

e. *Medications.* Remind patients to bring a list of any medications they currently take. Usually patients are asked not to bring in the actual medications. The list should include the name, use, and dosage of each current medication. This will make you an angel in the eyes of the other caregivers, who will receive a list rather than a grocery bag of various pills of generic appearance. Caregivers can then make sure that no medication is overlooked during the patient's stay.

f. *Special needs.* Ask the patient about any special needs, such as a walker, elevated toilet seat, cane, special diet, and/or room requirements. If you know about such requests in advance, you can be prepared and ready to handle them.

g. *Customer relations.* Reassure patients that your department or unit has a real interest in them and their special needs. This will make them feel that you truly care about their needs.

■ **verify:** *to validate insurance benefits and coverage; usually entails calling the specific insurance company and providing the patient's information*

This brief telephone contact has a multitude of advantages. You can **verify** insurance coverage prior to admission. You can inform the care team of any special needs or arrangements for this patient before his or her arrival. Probably the most important result is the reassurance you provide to patients that they are important, that their arrival is expected, and that your unit will be prepared for them.

■ **facesheet:** *chart form used for identification of patient. Includes patient's name, address, Social Security number, hospital numbers, physician(s), employer information, and insurance information*

2. The next step is to assemble the chart forms. Most institutions use some variation of all of the following forms:
   ■ **Facesheet**
   ■ Consent to treatment
   ■ Release of information
   ■ Charging system
   ■ Consultation forms
   ■ Admission physical assessment form
   ■ Daily documentation forms
   ■ Graphic forms
   ■ Patient teaching forms
   ■ Ordering sheets
   ■ Progress notes
   ■ Copies of information from other institutions or transfer forms

Figure 3–1 shows a typical example of the contents of one hospital patient chart.

Preparing the chart in advance avoids the need to grab forms in front of an already anxious or annoyed patient. It also acts as a doublecheck system to ensure that you complete all forms needed for your facility. Figure 3–2 is one example of a hospital procedure for putting together an admission chart.

Facesheet
Attestation
Coding summary
Patient property record
Patient instructions
Dictated history and physical
Autopsy (if done)
Dictated consultations
Physician orders
Medication records
Special forms as indicated for patient: • Cardiac catheterization records • Electrophysiology lab reports • Cardiovascular lab data • Emergency records • Op-patient records • Procedure reports • Prenatal records • Delivery records • Anesthesia records • Pathology reports
Electrocardiology reports
Therapy reports: • Physical therapy • Occupational therapy • Speech and hearing therapies
Treatment plans
Respiratory therapy
Charge sheets
Consents
Living wills
Patient clinical pathways
Patient teaching tools
Nutritional evaluations
Cumulative data graphs
Daily nursing documentation
Code status
Nursing discharge records

Figure 3–1   Sample hospital chart contents

PROCEDURE TITLE:	Admission Packet Assembly
DEFINITION:	An *admission packet* is a collection of both medical record and financial forms that must be either reviewed or completed at the time the patient is admitted to the hospital.
PURPOSE:	To provide instruction about the completion of an admission packet.
SCOPE:	This procedure applies to all health unit coordinators and team care specialists associated with patient focused care units. This also applies to the following central departments: Intake, Patient Financial Services, and Ambulatory Surgery.
CONTENTS:	How to build an admission packet and how to process the packet at preadmission and admission.

PROCEDURE:

1. An admission packet will be assembled either after a preadmission call is made or after an admission interview.

2. The health unit coordinator will generate the following:
   * Facesheet
   * Labels
   * **addressograph plate**

3. The health unit coordinator will make a wristband for the patient by inserting a label into a wristband.

4. The health unit coordinator will gather the following forms for the packet and affix labels to the forms:
   * Facesheet
   * Consent to treatment
   * Refusal of consent to treatment
   * Consent to release of information
   * Pediatric questionnaire, if applicable

5. The health unit coordinator will highlight the following on the facesheet:
   a. Any missing information
   b. Any information that must be verified

6. The items gathered in items 2–5 will be processed as follows:
   At preadmission:
   a. All necessary forms are placed in a plastic holder.
   b. Packets are filed alphabetically by day of admission.
   At admission:
   a. Complete any paperwork.
   b. Copy insurance cards (front and back).
   c. Separate and process financial forms.
   d. Complete chart assembly and deliver to health care team.

Figure 3–2 Sample hospital chart contents

■ *addressograph plate:*
plastic card used to imprint patient name and hospital identification number on all chart forms

▨ PROCESSING THE CHART

Once the chart is assembled, the only missing piece is the patient. When the patient arrives and goes through the admission process discussed in Chapter 4, the chart plays a vital role in his or her health care. A very important part of processing the chart includes **coding** the patient's condition for reimbursement purposes. This process involves looking at not only the patient's general diagnosis, but also any other concurrent health problem or **comorbidities** that may increase the cost of care. For example, a patient may be in your hospital because of congestive heart failure. By looking at the patient's treatment record and participating in the patient's health care conferences with the other members of the health care team and the physician, you may discover other additional problems, such as **hypokalemia**, that can change the DRG coding of the record and increase cost-of-care reimbursement. You can learn this coding process by using computer-assisted modules or at many postsecondary schools.

Processing the chart takes a knowledge of the requirements for the complete medical record. Figure 3–3 is an example of one hospital's policy regarding completion of the medical record. All facilities develop their own policies according to the recommendations and regulations of the **Joint Commission on Accreditation of Healthcare Organizations (JCAHO)**, the state board of health, and recommendations from **Medicare**.

■ **coding:** method of assigning a specific number to a disease state to identify reimbursement amounts; used for insurance coverage from Medicare and some commercial insurance companies

■ **comorbidities:** additional diseases or illnesses associated with a specific patient coexisting with the patient's initial admission diagnosis

■ **hypokalemia:** low amounts of an electrolyte (potassium) in the body

■ **Joint Commission on Accreditation of Healthcare Organizations (JCAHO):** private (nongovernmental) organization that monitors hospitals for standards of practice and care

■ **Medicare:** health insurance coverage from the government for citizens aged 65 and older

I. GENERAL REQUIREMENTS

The information contained in the medical record shall serve to identify the patient, support the diagnosis, justify treatment rendered, and accurately document the results of this treatment. Generally, the medical record will contain the following informational items:

A. Identification of the patient (facesheet)
B. Medical history
C. Report of physical examination
D. Progress notes indicating results of treatment
E. Reports of radiological, laboratory, and other specialized diagnostic and therapeutic procedures (appropriate signatures required)
F. Reports of operative procedures, if performed
G. Report of any consultations
H. Physician orders
I. Observation notes of nursing service and other ancillary service associates
J. Clinical résumé
K. Indication of final diagnoses, complications, and operative procedures
L. Appropriate consents

II. SIGNATURES

A. All entries in the medical record shall be dated and authenticated by signature.
B. Handwritten:
1. If the physician desires to use a signature stamp, written authorization shall be obtained from the hospital chief executive officer per policy.
2. With the exception of progress notes, all entries by a medical student shall be countersigned by a member of the house staff or the attending physician.
3. Physicians may sign for each other when there is evidence in the record that the "signing" physician had sufficient knowledge of the patient and the situation to assume responsibility for authenticating the order.

continues

Figure 3–3 Sample hospital policy for completing the medical record

III. APPLICABLE MEDICAL RECORD FORMS AND
DOCUMENTATION REQUIREMENTS
  A. Registration sheet
  B. Discharge summary (clinical résumé)
        The clinical résumé should be dictated upon discharge of the patient
     from the hospital. This résumé should briefly recapitulate the significant
     findings and events of the patient's hospitalization. His/her condition
     on discharge and recommendations and arrangements for future care
     are included. The résumé should specifically document the following:
     1. Reason for hospitalization
     2. Significant findings
     3. Procedures performed and treatment rendered
     4. Condition of patient on discharge
     5. Pertinent instruction regarding
        a. Physical activity
        b. Medication
        c. Diet
        d. Follow-up care
     A final progress note may satisfy this provision in the case of
     uncomplicated deliveries, normal newborn infants, and patients with
     problems of a minor nature who require less than a forty-eight hour
     period of hospitalization.
  C. Autopsy report
        In the event of the death of the patient, when an autopsy is
     performed, a provisional anatomic diagnosis should be recorded in the
     medical record within three days. The final completed and signed
     report shall be made a part of the record within ninety days.
  D. Physician's orders
        Diagnostic and therapeutic orders shall be recorded, dated, and
     authenticated on this record.
  E. Reports of diagnostic and therapeutic procedures
        Pathology, radiology, laboratory, and reports of other diagnostic and
     therapeutic procedures shall be completed promptly and authenticated
     by the appropriate specialist.
  F. Report of history and physical examination
        A complete history and physical examination shall be documented
     within twenty-four hours of admission and prior to surgery. If the report
     is dictated, a note to this effect shall be made in the record with
     pertinent remarks concerning the provisional diagnosis and condition of
     the patient.
     The history shall include:
     1. Chief complaint
     2. Details of present illness
     3. Inventory of body systems
     4. Allergies/medication reactions
     5. Medications (including dosages)
        The physical exam shall include pertinent findings resulting from a
     comprehensive assessment of all systems of the body and a statement
     of conclusions/impressions and course of action planned during the
     patient's hospitalization.
        An interval history and physical note documenting current vital signs
     and changes in the patient's condition subsequent to this history and
     physical are acceptable if accompanied by a legible copy of a history
     and physical exam recorded by a member of the medical staff within a

continues

Figure 3–3   Continued

period of thirty days prior to admission or surgery. The interval history and physical note are documented within seven days prior to admission or surgery.

G. Progress notes

Pertinent progress notes shall be recorded at the time of observation, sufficient to permit continuity of care and transferability. Wherever possible, each of the patient's clinical problems or changes should be clearly identified in the progress notes and correlated with specific orders as well as results of tests and treatment. Opinions requiring medical judgment should be written or authenticated only by the authorized house staff members and individuals who have been granted clinical privileges. Progress notes shall be written at least daily on critically ill patients, and those for whom there is difficulty in diagnosis or management of the clinical problem. A final progress note shall be written on the day of discharge. In the event of death, the final progress notes shall indicate the events leading to and suspected cause of death.

H. Consultations

Report of a consultation should indicate an examination of the patient and a review of the patient's medical record. The report shall include pertinent findings as well as the opinions and recommendations of the consultant. In cases involving surgery, except in emergency situations, the consultation note should be recorded prior to surgery.

I. Preoperative note

A preoperative note, which includes the preoperative diagnosis, shall be recorded in the progress notes and signed by the surgeon prior to surgery.

J. Surgery record

Completion of this form is the responsibility of the surgery department. Required data includes:
- Date
- Pre-op diagnosis
- Procedure
- Type of anesthesia
- Operating staff
- Special equipment used
- Room and time of service
- Units of blood used

K. Anesthesia records

1. Pre-anesthetic note: A pre-anesthesia evaluation of the patient will be recorded by an anesthesiologist with appropriate documentation of pertinent information relative to a choice of anesthesia and surgical or obstetrical procedures anticipated. This evaluation should include the patient's previous drug history, other anesthesia experiences, and any potential anesthesia problems.

2. Comments relative to events taking place during induction, maintenance, and emergence from anesthesia shall be documented on the anesthesia record.

3. The level of the patient's consciousness and authorization for release of the patient from the recovery room shall be documented on the recovery room record. The release order shall be recorded on the physician's order sheet.

4. Post-anesthetic note: The anesthesiologist will record a post-anesthetic note describing the presence or absence of anesthesia-

continues

Figure 3–3   *continued*

related complications. This note shall also include the signature of the anesthesiologist and shall specify the date and time of the notation. A similar note, including the date and time, is required when a patient leaves the post-anesthesia recovery area.
 L. Operative report
   The operative report shall be completed immediately following the surgical procedure and shall contain a description of the finding, a detailed account of the techniques used and tissues removed or altered, a postoperative diagnosis, and the names of the primary and any assisting physicians.
 M. Consent
   An informed surgical consent shall be obtained and documented in the medical record prior to the performance of a surgical or other medical procedure.
 N. TNM staging form
   This form is utilized to document the staging of tumors in cancer patients. It is the responsibility of the surgeon to complete this form.

Figure 3–3   *continued*

Any other form that is used in your facility should also be addressed in your medical record policy and procedure. Some examples of other forms that may be used include:

- Obstetrical records
- Newborn records
- Short-stay records
- Outpatient records
- Transfer records

COMMUNICATING WITH THE MEDICAL RECORDS DEPARTMENT

A strong communication link must be maintained with your central medical records department. **Reimbursement** rules from commercial payers and state and federal sources change rapidly, and you will need a reliable, constant resource who will share this information with you. Changes in chart forms and ways of processing records will constantly occur; only by working closely with this department will you be up-to-date with the latest revisions. Many institutions have established timeframes for meetings with the central departments. Figure 3–4 is an example of one such meeting agenda from a hospital that established weekly meetings with a representative from the health unit coordinators and a representative from the central medical records department of the hospital. They established a consistent agenda to encourage the sharing of changes in reimbursement guidelines and hospital forms.

- **reimbursement:** *payment to a facility in return for services provided to a patient; usually from insurance carriers or government programs*

Medical Records and Health Care Representative Meeting
Date:_____

Present:
AGENDA
 1. New hospital forms
 2. Changes in hospital forms

continues

Figure 3–4   Sample agenda for meeting between representatives of health unit coordinators and medical records department

3. Changes in state or local regulations for reimbursement
4. Any specific changes in commercial insurance requirements
5. Medical Records Department:
   • How charts are reviewed once they return to the central department, including any specific criteria used for review
   • Any noted problems with charts coming to the central department after discharge
6. Health Care Representative:
   • Any new problems with maintaining records or finding needed information
7. Time to share new ideas for continued success.

Figure 3–4 *continued*

Following this meeting, the participants returned to their peers and shared what they had learned. This allowed an avenue for both groups to get to know each other better and to identify problems and resolve them as soon as possible.

CONCURRENT ANALYSIS

Concurrent analysis is a system of reviewing the patient's chart on a daily basis, looking for opportunities to improve the recordkeeping system. As mentioned earlier, appropriate DRG coding of the medical record can change the reimbursement opportunities greatly. As the patient's condition changes, so will the coding. This also provides a time to review the chart for appropriate signatures and forms. By looking at the chart daily, you will discover the expected date of discharge. Many of the discharge steps can be started before the actual date of departure, such as ensuring that arrangements are being made for durable home health needs like oxygen or assistive devices for ambulation. Figure 3–5 is an example of a worksheet for concurrent analysis.

ROUTINE MAINTENANCE OF CHARTS

If concurrent analysis is done daily, chart maintenance becomes a snap. The most time-consuming task will be thinning charts, as they become too thick to handle easily and make finding current patient data too time-consuming. A procedure for thinning the record appears in Appendix B.

Chart ID Number: _____

Criteria	Initials/date	Initials/date	Initials/date	Initials/date	Initials/date	Initials/date	Initials/date	Initials/date
Signatures needed tagged								
Facesheet checked								
H&P checked for coding updates								
Orders completed								
Test results on chart								

Figure 3–5 Concurrent analysis of medical records

The following checklist may be used in daily maintenance of charts:

1. Replenish any needed forms (you should have at least enough for the next day):
   - Physician order sheets
   - Progress notes
   - Nursing notes
   - Vital sign records
   - Documentation forms for allied health team members (physical therapy, respiratory therapy, dietitians, speech and/or occupational therapists, etc.)
2. Evaluate the record to see if it needs to be thinned.
3. Check for labs results, x-ray reports, and similar items to be posted on the chart.

ADVANCE DIRECTIVES

Advance directives are written instructions about decision making for medical treatment if patients are unable to speak for themselves. These directives state the patient's preferences regarding medical treatment and identify who should make those treatment choices if the patient is unable to make such decisions because of medical or mental incapacitation. There are basically four types of advance directives: living will, statement on life-prolonging procedures, appointment of a health care representative, and durable power of attorney for health care.

Living Will

A *living will* is a declaration by a patient to his or her own physician stating the patient's desire that the dying process not be artificially prolonged. These provisions can apply only to a person suffering from a condition from which there is no hope of recovery, when death is expected.

Life-Prolonging Procedures

Instructions regarding life-prolonging procedures are executed by an individual to tell health care providers that all available means should be used to extend that individual's life, regardless of the prognosis.

Health Care Representative

A document appointing a health care representative designates a specific individual to make health care decisions for the patient should the patient become unable to participate in discussions and decisions relating to his or her own health care needs.

Durable Power of Attorney for Health Care

A *durable power of attorney for health care* is a written document that names a specific individual to act on behalf of the patient. The document must be notarized (signed in the presence of a notary public). This document may also give authority for financial and other personal matters. This type of document should be completed before the patient is admitted to the hospital.

Most hospitals require patients to make some form of advance directive, either before or at the time of admission. Check your facility for specific forms and policies for this procedure.

REVIEW QUESTIONS

Multiple Choice Questions

1. When calling patients to obtain information prior to their admission to the hospital, what information do you want to know?
   a. Reason for hospitalization
   b. Name of physician
   c. Insurance carrier
   d. All of these

2. You can verify insurance coverage by which of the following methods?
   a. Ask patients if their insurance is valid
   b. Look at the insurance card
   c. Call the insurance company
   d. All of these

3. Concurrent analysis should be done:
   a. daily.
   b. weekly.
   c. upon discharge.
   d. prior to patient arrival.

4. Discharge arrangements are made:
   a. at the time of discharge.
   b. as soon as need is identified.
   c. by the patient's family.
   d. only by request of the patient.

5. Which of the following types of forms may be thinned from a medical record?
   a. Physician order sheets
   b. Nursing notes

   c. Progress notes
   d. All of these

6. The type of advance directive that tells the medical team to use all possible means to extend life, regardless of prognosis, is the:
   a. living will.
   b. life-prolonging procedures statement.
   c. health care representative appointment.
   d. health care power of attorney.

7. The central medical records department can help you:
   a. keep abreast of new chart forms.
   b. update you on insurance changes.
   c. keep track of common problems with charts sent to that department.
   d. all of these.

8. The chart form that has the patient's name, address, Social Security number, physician information, and insurance information is the:
   a. facesheet.
   b. order sheet.
   c. history and physical sheet.
   d. all of these.

True/False Questions

9. T F Comorbidities are documented to increase reimbursement by the payer.

10. T F The patient's chart is a legal document.

SUGGESTED LEARNING ACTIVITIES

1. Obtain as many record forms as possible used in your own or a local facility. Describe their use in the medical record.

2. Illustrate the difference between coding, concurrent analysis, and routine chart maintenance.

3. Have each student write an advance directive and then share them with each other.

Patient Admission and Discharge

After reading this chapter, you will be able to:

- *Admit a patient.*
- *Admit observation patients.*
- *Transfer a patient.*
- *Discharge a patient.*

OVERVIEW

The most important fact to keep in mind as you begin a patient's admission process is that you are generally the first person the client interacts with. Not only do you *represent* the hospital, you *are* the hospital to the individual patient during the admission process. This chapter cannot prepare you to handle all the situations you may encounter while admitting or discharging a patient, but the information in this chapter will enable you to modify procedures as needed, such as communicating to the client and all caregivers, clarifying expectations of all involved, and caring for the comfort and physical needs of the patient. You need to master the interpersonal skills discussed in Chapter 2.

This chapter covers policy and procedures dealing with the admission process, including the observation client (admitted for a defined period of time as determined by individual hospitals), the internal transfer process, transfer to another facility, and the discharge process. Flowcharts are included to aid in developing a work-flow pattern.

COMMUNICATION PLAN

A communication plan between the physician's office and the hospital makes the patient's entry into the hospital setting as smooth as possible. Communication technology permits immediate transfer of information that avoids duplication of questions and testing. A transmittal by fax machine or computer enables you to anticipate the patient's needs and begin the paper trail for the patient's entry into the hospital system. Figure 4–1 is an example of a format for communication between the physician's office and the hospital.

The fax communication process is meant to prevent duplication of effort by staff. Patients become very annoyed when asked the same questions by multiple people; for some patients, the repetition can be very tiring. By recording the information on the fax sheet, the chances for errors of omission and misunderstandings are reduced. The format also allows staff to use it as a check sheet so that nothing is forgotten. The fax format, therefore, must be designed with the organization's needs in mind. Collaboration between the physician's office and the hospital is necessary in order to have customer satisfaction remain high.

From: Physician's Office _____
    Telephone _____ FAX Number _____

Please Check Appropriate Patient Status
_____Inpatient Admission _____Outpatient Procedure _____Outpatient Surgery
_____23 Hour Observation _____Short Stay Chemo

DATE OF SERVICE: _____Medical Record # _____

Patient's Name _____ Sex _____

Home Phone _____Work Phone _____Date of Birth _____

Admitting MD _____Other MD _____Person Scheduling _____

Diagnosis _____ICD9 _____

1. Member's Name _____ Employer _____

2. Policy # _____ Social Security # _____

3. Member's Name _____ Employer _____

4. Policy # _____ Social Security # _____

	Primary	Secondary
Insurance		
Precert Number		
Length of Stay		
Phone Number		
Insurance Contact		

Office Precert _____Hospital Precert _____None Needed _____

OUTPATIENTS ONLY

Procedures and Tests
CT _____ Bone Scan _____
Ultrasound _____ Diagnostic X-Ray _____
Doppler _____ Mammo _____
Treadmill _____ EEG _____ Echo _____
EMG _____ Labs _____
MRI _____ Other _____
PREP _____

DATE FAX RECEIVED BY:

DATE SCHEDULE BY:

Figure 4–1   Patient intake fax sheet

▬▬ ADMISSION PROCESS

A patient may begin the admission process in a variety of ways. Possible entry points include:

1. Scheduled admission
2. Admission from the emergency department
3. Admission as "23-hour observation"
4. Transfer from another unit
5. Transfer from another facility

The hospital needs to identify the many potential entry points by which a patient may access the facility. The most common access point available to a patient for admission is through the physician's office. A physician's office staffer calls the hospital to reserve a bed for the patient. Generally, there is a single point of contact for the office to call, but in some cases the office staff needs to call the specific area in the hospital that serves the patient's primary needs or diagnosis. Either way, the first step is for the physician's office staff to initiate contact with the hospital. If the patient is going to be an inpatient, the patient is assigned to the correct inpatient area based on the diagnosis.

Ideally, when the hospital is notified of a patient admission, a hospital health care representative calls the patient at home to discuss the admission procedure. This representative may be you, or it may be a nurse, depending on the hospital procedure. This enables patients to be introduced to the hospital prior to admission and allows them to feel that they know someone on the unit before admission. It is expected that any anxiety the patient may be feeling can be reduced by this process.

One concern patients have in today's health care environment relates to financial responsibility. By verifying the insurance coverage prior to admission, the patient can control health care decisions and focus on health-related issues rather than financial concerns. The institution can verify insurance coverage and rectify any problems in a proactive manner.

A second concern that is reduced by this prehospitalization phone call is providing for special needs a patient may have while in the hospital. The Americans with Disability Act (ADA) assures individuals with disabilities the right to access health care that provides those persons with appropriate accommodations. Unfortunately, there have been instances when the accommodation was not made. For example, an individual with hearing impairment was not provided an interpreter before signing an informed consent. In another case, a child was put into a hospital bed and the wheelchair was taken away but the child needed the wheelchair for mobility. These problems and many others can be eliminated when communication takes place prior to the hospitalization, to ensure that the hospital can provide reasonable accommodations.

Once the patient arrives at the hospital, you provide the initial greeting. Remember that you are representing the hospital and yourself. The patient should be introduced to the health care team and encouraged to be an active participant on the health care team if his or her condition allows for that participation. Figure 4–2 summarizes a general admission process.

Alternative Admission Processes

In addition to being admitted from the physician's office or home to the hospital, the patient may be admitted from an outpatient area to the inpatient area. If the patient had outpatient surgery and needs to become an inpatient because of complications, much of the paperwork may already be completed. Your primary role is to identify information that must still be provided, such as insurance verification. One example of the difference in your role in this circumstance is shown in Figure 4–3. Variations of this flowchart may be identified at individual hospital settings.

The internal patient transfer process is another means of admitting a patient. This process is most often used when a patient is transferred from intensive care

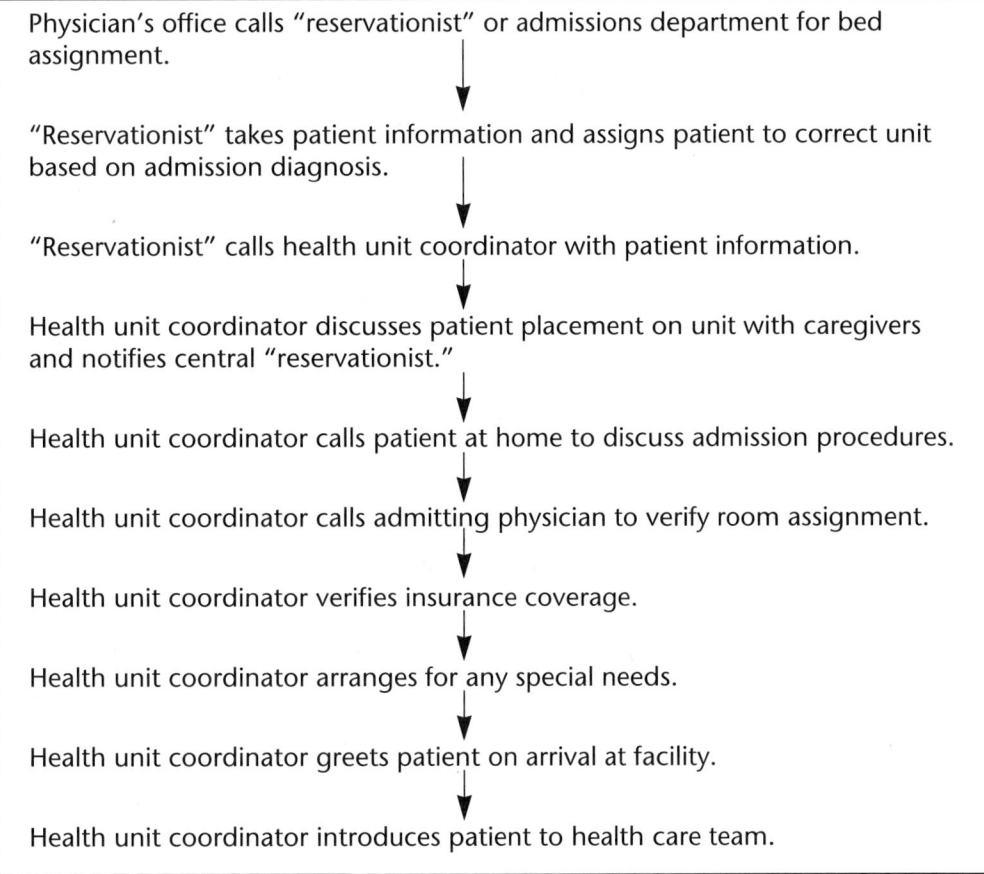

Physician's office calls "reservationist" or admissions department for bed assignment.

"Reservationist" takes patient information and assigns patient to correct unit based on admission diagnosis.

"Reservationist" calls health unit coordinator with patient information.

Health unit coordinator discusses patient placement on unit with caregivers and notifies central "reservationist."

Health unit coordinator calls patient at home to discuss admission procedures.

Health unit coordinator calls admitting physician to verify room assignment.

Health unit coordinator verifies insurance coverage.

Health unit coordinator arranges for any special needs.

Health unit coordinator greets patient on arrival at facility.

Health unit coordinator introduces patient to health care team.

Figure 4–2   General admission process flowchart

to another unit or from a general unit to intensive care. The transfer is initiated through a physician's written order. Some hospitals do not staff all the points of entry for a patient 24 hours a day. Therefore, it is important to call the receiving unit to verify that the admitting area is open. Once a contact is made on the receiving unit, the request for transfer is generally done by means of a computer system. The receiving unit checks if a bed is available for the patient and, if there is, assigns the bed. A representative of the health care team from the requesting unit will provide a patient care report to the receiving unit. The patient is then transferred. Figure 4–4 is an example of the decision-making tree for an internal transfer process.

The patient may also require transfer to another facility. This transfer may be due to a medical need, an insurance request, or the patient's request. The transfer is initiated by the physician's written order. You must notify discharge planning/social services to make sure the hospital is meeting its obligation of care. The importance of careful completion of all appropriate forms cannot be overemphasized. The patient's continuity of care depends on the communication efforts supported by accurate completion of all transfer forms. Procedure 1 sets out the steps for transfer of a patient to another facility. The individual record contents required for transferring a patient depend on the policy and procedures of your facility as well as external regulations. For example, an external regulation relating to extended care facilities states that documentation of the patient receiving a purified protein derivative skin test (PPD) within the past three months must be included in transfer documents for an extended care facility. This is a safeguard related to potential tuberculosis exposure.

Did the patient come directly to the unit?

NO	YES
↓	↓
Admit patient.	Patient escorted to unit by info desk personnel.
↓	↓
Reprint facesheet when patient arrives.	Patient introduced to staff.
↓	↓
Arrange chart in discharge order.	Review facesheet with patient.
↓	↓
Review deficient information.	Admit patient.
↓	↓
Remove all financial forms.	Review deficient information.
↓	↓
Leave admission name plate at desk.	Place wristband on patient.
	↓
	Copy insurance cards.
	↓
	Obtain consent signatures.
	↓
	Discuss advance directives.
	↓
	Escort patient to bed.
	↓
	Place name plate in holder.
	↓
	Assemble patient chart.
	↓
	Verify additional insurance.
	↓
	Obtain certifications.
	↓
	Identify financial arrangement needs.
	↓
	Follow up on any deficient information.

Figure 4–3   Admission process flowchart

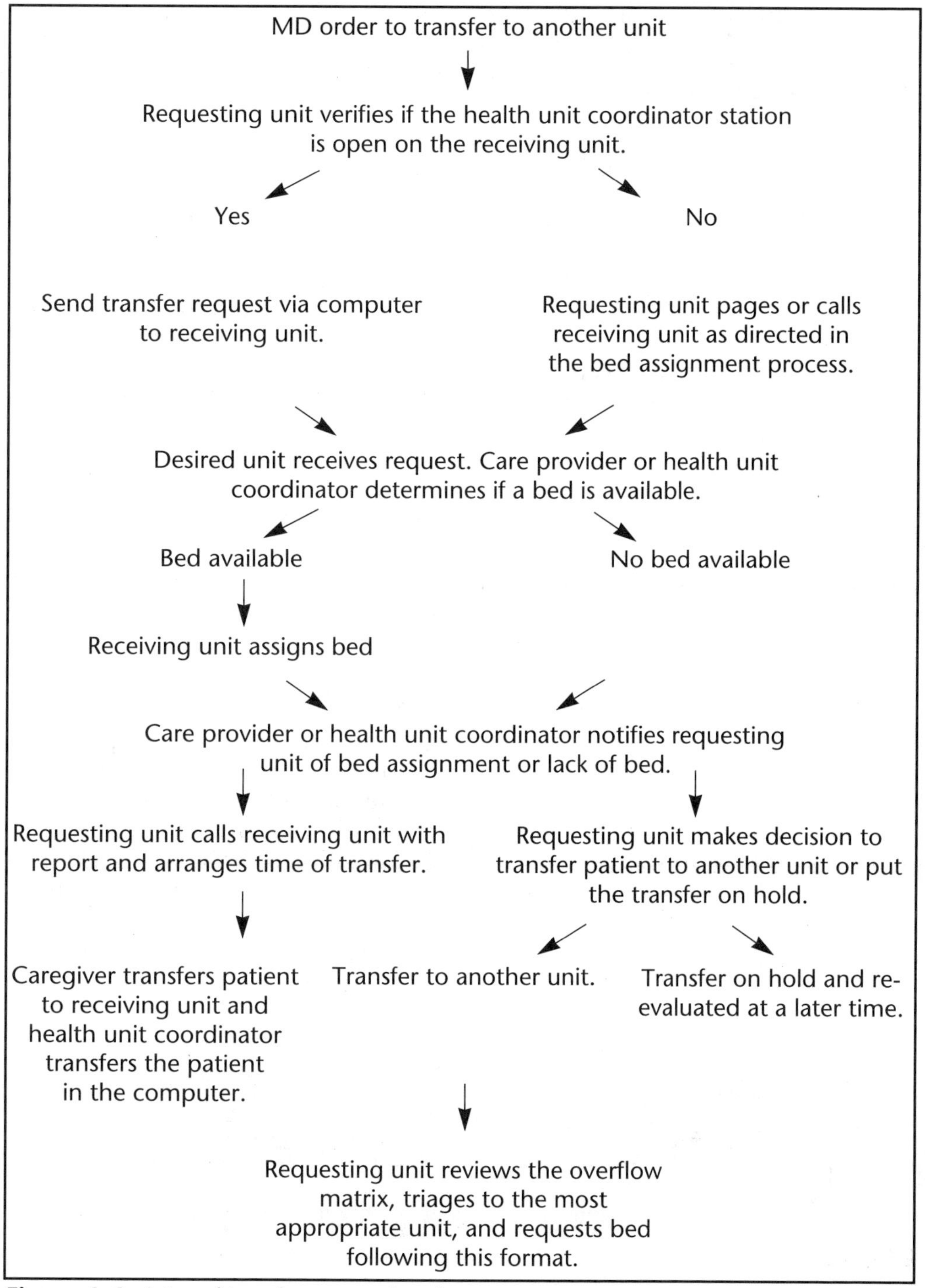

MD order to transfer to another unit

Requesting unit verifies if the health unit coordinator station is open on the receiving unit.

Yes   No

Send transfer request via computer to receiving unit.

Requesting unit pages or calls receiving unit as directed in the bed assignment process.

Desired unit receives request. Care provider or health unit coordinator determines if a bed is available.

Bed available   No bed available

Receiving unit assigns bed

Care provider or health unit coordinator notifies requesting unit of bed assignment or lack of bed.

Requesting unit calls receiving unit with report and arranges time of transfer.

Requesting unit makes decision to transfer patient to another unit or put the transfer on hold.

Caregiver transfers patient to receiving unit and health unit coordinator transfers the patient in the computer.

Transfer to another unit.

Transfer on hold and re-evaluated at a later time.

Requesting unit reviews the overflow matrix, triages to the most appropriate unit, and requests bed following this format.

Figure 4–4   Internal transfer process flowsheet

PROCEDURE

1   TRANSFER TO ANOTHER FACILITY

1. Care team verifies the discharge orders.
2. Care team notifies the health unit coordinator of the pending discharge.

3. Notify discharge planning/social service if the patient needs any home health support or is being transferred to a facility other than the

continues

P R O C E D U R E   1   continued

home. Assessment and discharge services are also available to all Medicare patients at this time.

4. Complete the patient transfer-discharge record.

5. Copy all requested forms and place in an envelope.

6. Use a checklist to indicate the contents of the envelope. Potential contents include:

   ■ chest x-ray

   ■ transfer form

   ■ PPD note (purified protein derivative skin test)

   ■ facesheet

   ■ discharge summary

   ■ consultations

   ■ diagnostic tests

   ■ nursing notes

   ■ physician orders and progress notes

7. Return all forms to the correct sections of the patient's chart after copying is completed.

8. Complete financial counseling.

9. Arrange for required transportation.

10. Assist in the transfer of patients from the unit to waiting transportation.

■■■■ OBSERVATION PATIENT

A patient may be admitted to the hospital as an *observation patient*. (See Procedure 2.) It is important to know the hospital's policy concerning observation patients. If your facility's policy states that a patient may be classified as an observation patient for 48 hours, it is imperative that the status be changed from observation to inpatient if the patient requires an additional stay. Otherwise, the hospital will not be reimbursed for the additional hospital stay. In addition, you will need to verify with the patient's insurance company an increase in the number of days approved for coverage.

P R O C E D U R E

2   OBSERVATION PATIENT ADMISSION

Admit an Observation Patient

1. Follow proper inquiry functions on the computer system.

2. Select proper patient identification from the series of choices.

3. Complete pathway, entering required information on each admission screen.

4. Enter the bed assignment for this patient (be sure to use available help screens behind each required field during this process).

Change an Observation Patient to an Inpatient

1. Obtain authorization from a representative of one of the following departments: Quality Review, Health Information Services, Patient Financial Services, or Patient Intake.

2. Ensure that an order has been written for an observation bed admission.

3. Proceed to Patient Functions Menu.

4. Complete the inpatient admit pathway as usual.

continues

PROCEDURE 2 *continued*

Change an Inpatient to an Observation Patient

1. Obtain authorization from a representative of one of the following departments: Quality Review, Health Information Services, Patient Financial Services, or Patient Intake.

2. Ensure that an order has been written for an observation bed admission.

3. *Warning:* Do not, under any circumstances, discharge the inpatient admission. Instead, proceed as follows:

4. Call reservations to have inpatient admission canceled. Be prepared to give the patient name, registration number, and name of the person who authorized the change.

5. Proceed to Patient Functions Menu.

6. Select appropriate portion of the Patient Admissions Menu.

7. Complete pathway, entering required information on each admission screen.

8. Enter the bed assignment for this patient (be sure to use available help screens behind each required field during this process). Refer to Figure 4–5 for a sample log to track inpatient-to-observation patient status.

Date	Time	Requestor	Department	Patient Name	Registration No.	Authorized by	Reason for change
							_____Original request and order do not match _____Payor denial for reimbursement _____Clerical error _____Other: attach explanation
							_____Original request and order do not match _____Payor denial for reimbursement _____Clerical error _____Other: attach explanation
							_____Original request and order do not match _____Payor denial for reimbursement _____Clerical error _____Other: attach explanation

Figure 4–5 Sample Inpatient to Observation log

▉ DISCHARGE PROCESS

Your role in the patient discharge process is extremely important. Once the physician orders the patient to be discharged, you need to notify the health care team responsible for the patient. You need to finalize the patient's financial arrangements with the hospital and notify the hospital's cashier if the patient is making a hospital payment. Analyze the chart to determine if all the pages have the appropriate signatures, patient identification, and physician and nursing documentation, and that all the lab reports are attached. Assemble the chart in the appropriate format for delivery to the medical records department. You may be responsible for coding the chart, or another specialist may do the coding and abstracting on the chart. Remember, the chart is a legal document and represents the care received by the patient. The chart must represent a complete picture of the hospitalization. Figure 4–6 is a flowchart representing a typical discharge process.

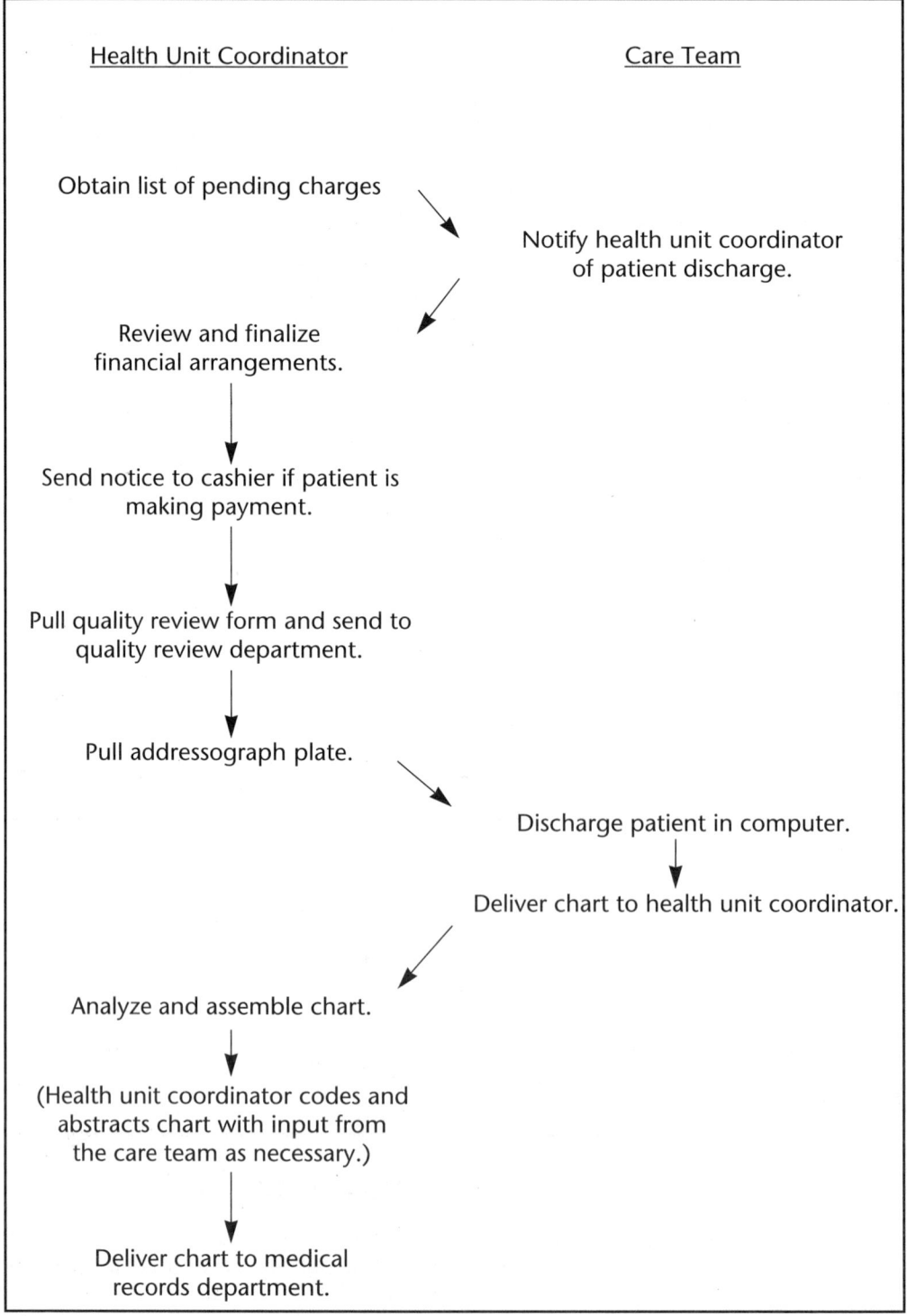

Figure 4–6   Discharge process flowchart

REVIEW QUESTIONS

Multiple Choice Questions

1. The patient may enter the inpatient hospital setting by:
   a. transferring from another facility.
   b. transferring from an outpatient area.
   c. referral from a physician's office.
   d. all of these.

2. Calling the patient at home prior to admission is helpful because:
   a. the hospital can prepare reasonable accommodation.
   b. financial concerns may be alleviated.
   c. patient anxiety may be reduced.
   d. all of these.

3. When transferring a patient to another facility, you should:
   a. allow the patient's family to make the arrangements.
   b. notify discharge planning/social services.
   c. follow the verbal direction of a physician.
   d. send only the discharge summary sheet with the patient.

4. When discharging a patient, the first thing you need to do is:
   a. verify the physician's order for discharge.
   b. arrange for transportation.
   c. make financial arrangements.
   d. move the patient to a waiting area.

5. An observation patient can:
   a. remain in the hospital as an observation patient for one week.
   b. be reclassified as an inpatient.
   c. stay in the emergency department for the observation stay.
   d. be reclassified at your discretion.

True/False Questions

6. T   F   The observation patient may stay in the hospital under this classification as long as treatment is needed.

7. T   F   Patients are responsible for making their own arrangements for any required accommodations.

8. T   F   Every transfer requires the same documentation effort.

SUGGESTED LEARNING ACTIVITIES

1. Admit patients, under supervision, who are scheduled admissions, emergency admissions, observation patients, and transfer patients (internal and external). Simulate the admission process before working with an actual patient population.

2. Monitor phone conversations during the preadmission process to gain a comfort level with communication techniques and questioning. Simulate this experience in a controlled setting before initiating a conversation with a patient.

3. Role-play situations involving patients with disabilities who are going through the admission process.

Financial Arranging

After reading this chapter, you will be able to:

Discuss financial arrangement options.

Identify guidelines for Medicare, Medicaid, and commercial insurance.

Determine primary and secondary insurances.

Understand the need for ongoing continuing education.

OVERVIEW

In your role as health unit coordinator, you become the person who knows if an individual patient has any financial needs. If complete coverage is not expected, what financial responsibility will the patient assume? What are some financial plans available at your facility? What types of payment plans can be accessed? Is there some charity coverage that might be available? To determine a plan for the patient, you will need to meet with the caregivers to determine possible total costs. If the patient is unable to discuss financial matters due to his or her physical condition, are there family or significant others who may be able to help link the patient to possible coverage?

Discussing financial concerns is not an easy task. It requires all of your tact and resources. Be prepared to discuss all options potentially open to the patient. Your goal is to learn all possible avenues for coverage while easing the patient's financial concerns. It is much kinder to look at possible solutions with the patient than to present the patient or family with a huge bill upon discharge.

In this chapter, you will find information and guidelines related to financial counseling. This includes initial assessment, discharge processing, out-of-pocket expenses, inpatient discharge approval, and self-pay negotiations. Insurance verification and the determination of primary and secondary insurance are discussed. Guidelines for Medicare, **Medicaid**, and commercial insurance are outlined. Changes in the rules and regulations governing financial counseling occur frequently, which makes it imperative for you to participate in ongoing continuing education and training. You need to be an active learner, seeking information and clarification.

■ **Medicaid:** *a federal health insurance plan, authorized by Title XIX of the Social Security Act (Public Law No. 89-97); administered by individual states to provide health care for the poor*

INITIAL FINANCIAL ASSESSMENT

The initial financial assessment for a patient is very important. It assesses the patient's level of insurance, self-pay resources, eligibility for public assistance, and the potential need for hospital assistance. The level of insurance assessment can be determined during the eligibility and benefits verification phone call. The call can be made prior to the patient's hospitalization if the admission is a planned admission.

Self-pay resources are evaluated taking into consideration the total household income before deductions, cash reserves, significant assets, and the number of household members. Evaluation of self-pay resources is very sensitive and must be completed in a respectful manner.

Public assistance screening is performed to determine if the patient is in need of and eligible for Medicaid. This is appropriate when a patient is financially unable to pay all or part of the hospital bill.

Most hospitals analyze their own resources to help patients pay for hospitalization as a last resort. Consideration and recommendation for hospital assistance is made only after exhausting all private funding and public assistance options, using the Self-Pay Allowance Income Scale as a guideline.

When the patient is discharged, the patient's anticipated out-of-pocket expense will be calculated and discharge approval will be determined as indicated in the following outline.

Inpatient Discharge Approval Outline

1. *A routine inpatient may be approved for discharge if the following conditions have been met:*
   - *All required forms have been signed*
                    and
   - *Anticipated out-of-pocket expense is less than $100*
                    OR
   - *Anticipated out-of-pocket expense is more than $100, the patient is not a candidate for public assistance and/or hospital assistance, and a deposit and/or suitable financial arrangements have been made*
                    OR
   - *Anticipated out-of-pocket expense is more than $100, the patient is a candidate for public assistance and/or hospital assistance, and discussions with the patient indicate the patient's willingness to cooperate in the application process.*
2. *Courtesy discharges may be allowed for acknowledged VIPs or if otherwise directed by the management.*
3. *A message to the cashier must be sent if either:*
   - *The patient will be making a deposit at discharge*
                    OR
   - *The patient deposited valuables with the cashier*

Financial arrangements for out-of-pocket expenses exceeding $100 and self-pay negotiations are outlined in Procedures 3 and 4. See Figure 5-1 for a sample calculation of a patient's out-of-pocket expenses.

Total charges	$4800.00
Less personal items	16.50
Less private room difference	0
Less deductible	250.00
Times co-insurance	20%
	- - - - - - - - -
	956.70
Plus personal items	16.50
Plus private room difference	0
Plus deductible (if $500 or more)	0
	- - - - - - - - -
Anticipated out-of-pocket	973.20

Figure 5-1 Calculating patient out-of-pocket expenses

PROCEDURE

3   FINANCIAL ARRANGEMENTS FOR OUT-OF-POCKET EXPENSES EXCEEDING $100

1. Explain to the patient or family member(s) how the anticipated out-of-pocket amount was calculated. Be sure to explain that this is an estimated amount.
2. Determine if the patient wishes to pay at discharge or if payment may be expected upon receipt of the bill.
3. If the patient wishes to pay at the time of discharge, instruct the patient or family to stop at the cashier's office before leaving the hospital. Notify the cashier of the patient's intent to pay and the amount to be paid.
4. If the patient states inability to pay upon discharge or receipt of bill, explain payment options, such as the 30/60/90-day plan.

5. If the payment plan is selected by a patient, thoroughly explain the conditions of the option selected and obtain all necessary signatures. Document the payment arrangement selection and forward the documentation to patient financial services.
6. Patients who absolutely refuse to discuss payment options at discharge or are unsure about the choice of payment options at discharge should be advised that they are expected to communicate with the hospital concerning any outstanding balance within 30 days of discharge.

PROCEDURE

4   SELF-PAY NEGOTIATIONS

1. If a patient is not covered by insurance, conduct an interview with the patient or family member(s) to determine appropriate resolution.
2. For patients who demonstrate the ability to pay, request a deposit and discuss the method for payment of the balance.
3. If the patient demonstrates an inability to pay, screen for public assistance programs, using the financial statement form.
4. After exhausting all private and public health care funding, screen for hospital assistance, using the Self-Pay Allowance Income Scale to

determine what recommendations should be made. If the patient qualifies for partial hospital assistance, the unaffected portion of the bill should be paid according to regular account payment procedures. Document the recommendation and notify the financial analyst in patient financial services for a review of the recommendation. The patient will receive written notification from patient financial services of the outcome of the assistance recommendation. Alert the financial analyst to any patient who could be a financial risk.

When the patient is discharged, anticipated out-of-pocket expense will be calculated and financial arrangements will be determined. Documentation regarding the patient's financial arrangements are to be recorded. Each entry must be dated and initialed. Discharge documentation should be forwarded to the billing department daily.

■ *certification:* review and approval of the necessity for and appropriateness of inpatient service

▮▮▮▮ INSURANCE CERTIFICATION

When identifying insurance **certification**, you need to identify not only the reason for hospitalization, but also any chronic conditions that may lengthen or alter the expected course of therapy. You may find that you need to discuss the primary diagnosis and potential chronic conditions with the nursing staff or case manager, in order to gain an understanding of the patient's condition, before calling for insurance certification. For example, if the patient is admitted for surgery but also has a history of diabetes, complications may arise because of the diabetes. You need to know the complete description of the procedure, history, and physical findings before you call the insurance company.

Many patients have coverage with more than one insurance company, so it is important to copy all insurance coverages. It is also important to know the policy for certification denial, so that you can develop a possible alternative plan.

The following list summarizes the insurance certification procedure:

1. Identify reason for hospitalization.
2. Identify any chronic conditions (diabetes, arthritis, etc.) that may lengthen or alter the expected course of therapy. These chronic conditions are not why the patient is being admitted. Talk with the caregivers on your unit if you are unclear as to possible complications.
3. Get complete descriptions of procedures or admission history and physical findings. When doing a precertification, tell the company all that you currently know about the patient and that you will need to call back as the need for other procedures occurs or develops when the patient actually arrives on your unit.
4. Copy all insurance coverages.
5. Anticipate the need for an alternative plan in the event of certification denial.

▄▄▄ MEDICARE

Medicare is a federal program with two parts. Part A pays for inpatient hospital care, inpatient care in a skilled nursing facility, home health care, and hospice care. Part B pays for physicians' services, outpatient hospital services, and durable medical equipment. Medicare pays for health care under the following conditions:

1. If you are 65 years of age or older.
2. If you are disabled.

Diagnostic Related Group (DRG): a dollar amount used by Medicare to pay hospitals for services rendered. It is based on the average of all patients belonging to a specific DRG adjusted for economic factors, inflation, and bad debts

Medicare is offered through the Social Security Administration of the Department of Health and Human Services (HHS). The amount of money paid is based on **Diagnostic Related Groups (DRGs)**.

Medicare is almost always a secondary payer under the following conditions:

1. A patient is under 65 and works for a company with more than 100 employees and has benefits.
2. A spouse of the patient is employed by an employer with more than 20 employees and has insurance.
3. The patient's problem is a work-related illness or injury and therefore eligible for workers' compensation.

Medicare's secondary payer status is the result of legislation passed by Congress in an effort to relieve the Medicare program of full financial responsibility for Medicare and hospital services provided to Medicare beneficiaries. A brief synopsis of the history of Medicare legislation is outlined here:

■ Omnibus Budget Reconciliation Act (OBRA) of 1980 made Medicare secondary to automobile, no-fault, and liability insurance.

■ OBRA 1981 made Medicare secondary to group insurance for people with insurance.

■ Tax Equity and Fiscal Responsibility Act (TEFRA) 1982 established working ages for employed beneficiaries and spouses aged 65 to 69.

■ Deficit Reduction Act (DEFRA) 1984 modified working ages by revising the minimum age for employed spouses of beneficiaries aged 65 to 69; spouses could be of any age under age 70.

■ COBRA 1985 modified working ages to current definition (eliminated age ceiling).

■ OBRA 1986 made Medicare secondary for disabled beneficiaries under age 65 (without end stage renal disease[ESRD]) covered under large group health plans (LGHPs).

■ OBRA 1990 extended disability provisions and ESRD coordination period.

■ OBRA 1993 eliminated concept of "active employee" in disability provision; modified rules concerning termination of ESRD coordination period.

Determination of Primary and Secondary Insurance

For appropriate billing to occur, it is necessary to correctly determine primary and secondary insurance coverage. Generally, the following rules are applied when you are trying to make that determination.

1. If the patient is employed and has group insurance, and the spouse also has group insurance that covers the patient, the primary payer is the patient's insurance and the secondary payer is the spouse's insurance.

2. If the patient is a minor child covered under multiple insurance plans, one of two rules will apply:
   a. Gender rule—dictates that father's insurance is primary and mother's insurance is secondary. Divorced parents may change this ruling.
   b. Birthday rule—dictates that insurance for parent whose birthday occurs first in the calendar year is primary. If both parents' birthdays are on the same day (birth year is not a consideration), the parent with the insurance that has been in effect the longest is the primary payer.

3. If the parents are divorced, the guidelines for determining primary payer may change as follows:
   a. Primary payer—insurance for parent with custody.
   b. Secondary payer—insurance for spouse of custodial parent.
   c. Tertiary payer—insurance for noncustodial parent. An exception to this rule occurs when the divorce decree gives the noncustodial parent responsibility for insurance and the insurance company knows of the decree.

4. Medicare is not always the primary payer. The circumstances under which Medicare is primary or secondary were discussed earlier.

5. CHAMPUS is secondary to all other plans except Medicaid and certain insurance policies designated as CHAMPUS supplements.

Unfortunately, the determination of primary and secondary insurance is sometimes complex, and you will need to verify your determination with an expert. When you are uncertain about applying the rules, seek assistance from peers and other experts in central department areas.

■ *CHAMPUS: Civilian Health and Medical Program of the Uniformed Services; a program administered by the Department of Defense that provides benefits for health care services furnished by civilian providers, physicians, and suppliers to spouses and children of active duty, retired, and deceased members of the armed forces*

▬▬▬ MEDICAID

Medicaid is a federal- and state-funded medical assistance program that pays for approved medical care for persons meeting certain assigned criteria. Eligibility criteria include:

1. Recipients of Aid to Dependent Children (AFDC)
2. Individuals receiving Federal Supplemental Security Income (SSI) meeting AFDC requirements
3. Pregnant women and newborns
4. Young children
5. 65 or older
6. Blind
7. Disabled
8. Qualified Medicare beneficiaries (persons entitled to Part A and meet other eligibility requirements)

Medicaid can pay for care three months before the month in which Medicaid application is made. Individuals may apply for Medicaid by sending applications to the county office, Division of Family and Children, Family and Social Services Administration, in the county where they reside, or a caseworker may be requested to assist in the application process. Medicaid eligibility must be verified each time a person is registered/admitted.

▨ COMMERCIAL INSURANCE

▪ *health maintenance organization (HMO):* *prepaid managed care plan in which the emphasis is on preventive and primary care. This care is provided by the "gatekeepers" in the system—family physicians, general practitioners, internists*

Commercial insurance can be either group or individual coverage. Managed care insurers manage delivery of health care, control costs by emphasizing primary and preventative care, and use quality assurance and utilization review to ensure appropriate delivery of care. Different types of managed care include **health maintenance organizations (HMOs)**, preferred provider organizations (PPOs), and point of service (POS). Precertification is required for most managed care plans, as is a document authorization number on payment approval.

HMO managed care emphasizes primary and preventative health care. PPOs contract with physicians and providers for negotiated fees. The physicians in a PPO follow quality assurance and utilization review procedures and do not bill for covered services. POS managed care is like other HMOs except that it allows self-referral to a specialist without primary care physician (PCP) authorization. There are significant annual deductibles and copays.

▨ WORKERS' COMPENSATION

Employers provide insurance coverage to employees who are injured or ill because of work. Federal, agricultural, and domestic employees are excluded, and coverage varies from state to state. File a workers' compensation claim only if the patient presents written verification upon admission, or call the employer to verify coverage. Document the name and address of the employer's compensation carrier as well as the date and time of injury or illness. Also document other insurance coverage.

▨ CHARITY CARE

Most hospitals have a policy or guideline to direct you in initiating the process required for charity care consideration. This is extremely important to the patient in need of health care who is unable to afford that care. You are generally the first person who can assess this need and therefore you become the advocate for your patient.

Generally, the following criteria must be met:
1. Hospital designates the maximum household income for any charity consideration. This can be independent or depend on the household size.
2. Financial statement is required.
3. Formal application must be completed.
4. Documentation of the financial information is provided by the guarantor.
5. Identify any potential assistance programs.
6. Identify any potential convertible assets.
7. Initiate a reasonable investigation.
8. Get formal approval. Authorization of an allowance for all or part of the outstanding debt is generally the responsibility of the financial manager/officer, who weights the facts of the case with reasonable judgment to reach an exception decision.

REVIEW QUESTIONS

Multiple Choice Questions

1. If your patient is hospitalized for a surgical intervention, it is important to:
   a. find out exactly what procedure is to be performed.
   b. find out the history of the patient.
   c. identify any chronic conditions the patient might have.
   d. all of these.
   e. none of these.

2. Documentation of financial arrangements:
   a. can be a verbal agreement with the patient.
   b. must be recorded, dated, and initialed.
   c. is completed by the insurance company.
   d. is between the physician and the patient.

3. Medicare is almost always a secondary payer when:
   a. the individual is over the age of 65.
   b. the patient is employed by a company with five or fewer employees.
   c. the illness or injury is work-related.
   d. the patient is disabled.

4. Some of the rules in determining which is primary or secondary insurance are:
   a. gender rule.
   b. birthday rule.
   c. the patient's insurance coverage is primary if the patient is employed and has group insurance.
   d. Medicare is not always a primary payer.
   e. all of these.

5. An example of a worker who may be entitled to workers' compensation is a:
   a. farmer.
   b. federal worker.
   c. domestic worker.
   d. hospital worker.

6. A routine inpatient may be approved for discharge if the following conditions have been met:
   a. all forms have been signed.
   b. out-of-pocket expense is less than $100.
   c. out-of-pocket expense is more than $100, the patient is a candidate for public assistance, and the patient will cooperate in the application process.
   d. all of these.

7. Medicare pays for health care when the:
   a. patient is under the age of 65.
   b. patient is disabled.
   c. patient is in financial need.
   d. patient has no insurance.

True/False Questions

8. T   F   When identifying insurance certification, you only need to identify the reason for the hospitalization.

9. T   F   Chronic conditions such as diabetes may lengthen the patient's expected hospital stay.

10. T   F   Medicare is always the primary payer.

SUGGESTED LEARNING ACTIVITIES

1. Evaluate the financial resources of a routine inpatient with commercial insurance coverage.

2. Collaborate with the health care team to identify chronic health conditions of patients requiring prolonged hospitalization.

3. Determine primary and secondary payers for patients who receive Medicare.

4. Simulate a charity care determination.

Discharge Planning

After reading this chapter, you will be able to:

Identify potential discharge options.

Prepare the medical record for patient discharge.

Identify resources needed to determine the patient's needs.

▰▰▰ OVERVIEW

Discharge planning begins at the time of a patient's admission. Today's health care environment has necessitated shortened hospital stays. The identification of discharge needs early in the patient's stay enables the hospital to ensure a smooth transition to other health care options. This phase of patient care is critical to the patient's customer satisfaction. The decision process that the patient and family may need to undertake is facilitated by your understanding of available options and financial constraints. The key to successful discharge planning is early involvement by the patient, family, and other health care team members.

You may or may not be working in a facility that uses official discharge planners. These health care professionals may come from a variety of educational backgrounds. Some discharge planners have a background in social work. These professionals typically have a master's degree in social work (MSW). Other discharge planners have their basic education in nursing. They are usually registered nurses (RNs) who have an associate's, baccalaureate, or master's degree. In some facilities, the discharge planner may have a background in case management.

You may also perform some discharge planning functions for patients. Regardless of who is assigned to perform these functions, the tasks for this role remain similar. You will be in an excellent position to know of patients who have discharge planning needs. As you admit the patients to your facility, you will become aware if they live alone, need financial assistance, or have any family resources to help upon discharge. By doing your concurrent analysis, you will discover each patient's health needs. For example, you may read in the physician progress notes that the patient will be discharged with a need for some durable health care equipment, such as oxygen or assistive devices. You may find out from talking with the other health care workers that a patient's condition is such that she will not be able to return to her own home and thus, at least temporarily, will need to find some transitional or extended care facility.

▰▰▰ DISCHARGE PLANNING NEEDS

The first step is to determine the need for financial assistance. Many agencies may provide financial support for your patients, as mentioned in Chapter 5. An additional concern for discharge planners is the patient's long-range needs. For example, if your patient is considered disabled as a result of his current health problems, he may be eligible for Social Security. This application process takes a fairly long time and the patient will be depending on you to start the process. Medicare and Medicaid applications may also have to be initiated because of your patient's health status.

Secondly, continuing health care needs require assistance. Often patients may come into your facility from home, but because of their changes in health status, they will not be able to return to their previous home situations. You may be called on to intervene for these patients. The following steps can help you and the health care team to determine the patient's need. The key is to learn as much about the patient as possible and consult with health care professionals.

1. Read the physician's progress notes for discharge plans and/or concerns in the patient's medical record.
2. Talk with the health care providers who are currently working with the patient, to determine the patient's abilities and disabilities in self-care.
3. Talk with all the health care workers involved in the patient's care. Has a physical or occupational therapist been seeing the patient? What would they recommend for continued support following discharge?
4. Talk with the patient. What are her expectations following discharge? Does she expect to return to the same level of functioning as before the episode of illness? Is she afraid of being alone and unable to care for her own needs? It is very frightening for the patient to feel that she is alone, without resources, or that people are planning her life without her input.
5. Talk with the family. What are their expectations? Be prepared to explain the needs the patient will have following discharge. It is a challenge to present these needs to a family and convey an open atmosphere for them to honestly tell you what they can and cannot provide. Some people may not be able to provide for all the needs of the client, but feel guilty or ashamed to tell you or the patient of their feelings or problems. Your patient's discharge care depends on knowing as much as possible about the needs and abilities of the family.

CARE OPTIONS

If it is decided that the patient will need continued care following discharge, there are a variety of options for placement. These options include, but are not limited to, the following care facilities.

Extended care facilities (ECFs) offer total care for the patient. These facilities usually require that patients be medically stable, even though they require more skilled care until their strength returns; or the patients may make this their new home.

These facilities usually offer some form of activity based on the patient's ability and may or may not provide rehabilitative services.

A *transitional care unit* or *subacute care unit* is usually selected to meet the short-term care needs of the patient who is still too ill to go home but is medically stable and will probably be able to return home after some rehabilitation and continued medical care. Typically, patients stay for two to six weeks in this type of facility.

A *rehabilitation facility* offers intensive physical and occupational therapy. These facilities are targeted to medically stable patients whose health care problems may or may not resolve. The focus is to teach them how to modify their lives to accommodate their limitations.

A *long-term acute care facility* provides more intensive health care to patients who have become medically stable and can be transferred out of the acute care facility. These patients may have been in the acute care facility for a month or longer, but still require a high level of care, although their conditions are fairly stable.

Home care options are a distinct possibility. Today more and more agencies provide a wide range of home care services. Agencies can provide services ranging from bathing, daily hygiene, and meals to specific treatments such as physical therapy, occupational therapy, speech therapy, oxygen therapy, intravenous therapy, and dialysis. Patient assessments are completed by a health team comprised of the professionals needed to plan, implement, and evaluate the care needed. The Visiting Nurse Association and various home health agencies provide services for the care of patients in their own homes.

Whichever level of care is determined to be necessary to meet the patient's health care needs, it is important for the health care team to discuss the options with the patient and/or family and significant others. Insurance coverage is a major consideration in determining care options, and the family needs resources to identify insurance decision points. Ultimately, the patient and/or family should make the final decision as to the patient's placement and provisions.

Once discharge plans have been made, don't forget about these details:
1. When is the patient expected to leave your facility?
2. How will the patient leave your facility (car, ambulance)?
3. Is there a need to arrange for durable medical equipment (oxygen, walker, etc)?

Finally, don't forget the individual. Let the patient know what to expect and when. If plans change, inform the patient as soon as possible. Try to let the family and/or significant others know as much as possible about the plans. Always provide the patient and family with a resource. Let them know who they can call if there is a problem or if additional help is required.

■■■ PREPARING THE MEDICAL RECORD FOR PATIENT DISCHARGE

At discharge, the medical record must be completed and put into a final form for recordkeeping. It is your responsibility to look at the record for any omissions of signatures and/or forms. As you prepare the record and note missing signatures, alert the appropriate people. If a physician needs to sign a particular form, how will you let him or her know this is needed? When, where, and how can he or she sign this in a timely and convenient manner? Most facilities tag the record where signatures are needed and place the record in a designated location. This may be at the health unit coordinator's station or in the medical records department. Check your facility's policy.

The medical record is then usually taken apart from the folder or chart. It may be scanned for electronic recordkeeping or filed in a special location within your facility. Follow the medical records policies of the facility where you work.

REVIEW QUESTIONS

Multiple Choice Questions

1. When admitting a patient, what discharge planning needs may be evident?
   a. Financial assistance
   b. Personal assistance
   c. Family resource
   d. All of these

2. The best option to meet short-term care needs of the patient who is too ill to return home but does not require acute care is:
   a. an extended care facility.
   b. a transitional care unit.
   c. long-term acute care.
   d. the family's home.

3. The patient's placement is decided by the:
   a. health unit coordinator.
   b. physician.
   c. patient.
   d. social worker.

4. The most likely placement option for the patient requiring intense physical therapy is:
   a. home care.
   b. an extended care facility.
   c. a rehabilitation facility.
   d. a long-term acute care facility.

5. The most likely placement option for patients who require care for the remainder of their lives is the:
   a. extended care facility.
   b. subacute care facility.

c. long-term acute care facility.

d. transitional care facility.

6. The person responsible for obtaining missing signatures on the chart is:

a. the nurse.

b. the medical records department.

c. the manager.

d. the health unit coordinator.

7. Resources that help you determine the patient's discharge care requirements include:

a. physicians' progress notes.

b. other health care providers.

c. the family.

d. all of these.

True/False Questions

8. T F   The first option to support a patient's discharge planning needs is the patient's family.

9. T F   Discharge planning can be done only at the time of discharge.

10. T F   Home health care options provide only nursing care.

SUGGESTED LEARNING ACTIVITIES

1. Collaborate with the health care team in identifying specific discharge needs of patients.

2. Make a list of facilities in your area that support discharge planning needs of patients. Identify expected communication patterns with each of these facilities and patient status requirements of each of the facilities.

3. Prepare the medical records chart for a patient's discharge. Validate protocols in your hospital setting.

Procedure Checklists

TRANSFER TO ANOTHER FACILITY

Competency will be considered obtained when the student has successfully completed at least five patient transfers to another facility. Successful completion of this procedure is determined by satisfactory performance of each step in this checklist. All steps must be performed to the satisfaction of the instructor.

	Needs practice	Satisfactory	Comments
1. Care team verifies the discharge orders.			
2. Care team notifies the health unit coordinator of the pending discharge.			
3. Notify discharge planning/social service if the patient needs any home health support or is being transferred to a facility other than the home. Assessment and discharge services are also available to all Medicare patients at this time.			
4. Complete the patient transfer-discharge record.			
5. Copy all requested forms and place in an envelope.			
6. Use a checklist to indicate the contents of the envelope. Potential contents include: ■ chest x-ray ■ transfer form ■ PPD note ■ facesheet ■ discharge summary ■ consultations ■ diagnostic tests ■ nursing notes ■ physician orders and progress notes			
7. Return all forms to the correct sections of the patient's chart after copying is completed.			

continues

PROCEDURE 1 CHECKLIST *continued*

	Needs practice	Satisfactory	Comments
8. Complete financial counseling.			
9. Arrange for required transportation.			
10. Assist in the transfer of patients from the unit to waiting transportation.			

PROCEDURE 2 CHECKLIST

OBSERVATION PATIENT ADMISSIONS

Competency will be considered obtained when the student has successfully completed at least five observation patient admissions. Successful completion of this procedure is determined by satisfactory performance of each step in this checklist. All steps must be performed to the satisfaction of the instructor.

	Needs practice	Satisfactory	Comments
Admit an Observation Patient			
1. Follow proper inquiry functions on the computer system.			
2. Select proper patient identification from the series of choices.			
3. Complete pathway, entering required information on each admission screen.			
4. Enter the bed assignment for this patient (be sure to use available help screens behind each required field during this process).			
Change an Observation Patient to an Inpatient			
1. Obtain authorization from a representative of one of the following departments: Quality Review, Health Information Services, Patient Financial Services, or Patient Intake.			
2. Ensure that an order has been written for an observation bed admission.			
3. Proceed to Patient Functions Menu.			
4. Complete the inpatient admit pathway as usual.			

continues

PROCEDURE 2 CHECKLIST *continued*

	Needs practice	Satisfactory	Comments
Change an Inpatient to an Observation Patient			
1. Obtain authorization from a representative of one of the following departments: Quality Review, Health Information Services, Patient Financial Services, or Patient Intake.			
2. Ensure that an order has been written for an observation bed admission.			
3. *Warning:* Do not, under any circumstances, discharge the inpatient admission. Instead, proceed as follows:			
4. Call reservations to have inpatient admission canceled. Be prepared to give the patient name, registration number, and name of the person who authorized the change.			
5. Proceed to Patient Functions Menu.			
6. Select appropriate portion of the Patient Admissions Menu.			
7. Complete pathway, entering required information on each admission screen.			
8. Enter the bed assignment for this patient (be sure to use available help screens behind each required field during this process). Refer to Figure 4–5 for a sample log to track inpatient-to-observation patient status.			

PROCEDURE 3 CHECKLIST

FINANCIAL ARRANGEMENTS FOR OUT-OF-POCKET EXPENSES EXCEEDING $100

Competency will be considered obtained when the student has successfully completed at least five financial arrangements. Successful completion of this procedure is determined by satisfactory performance of each step in this checklist. All steps must be performed to the satisfaction of the instructor.

	Needs practice	Satisfactory	Comments
1. Explain to the patient or family member(s) how the anticipated out-of-pocket amount was calculated. Be sure to explain that this is an estimated amount.			

continues

PROCEDURE **3** CHECKLIST *continued*

	Needs practice	Satisfactory	Comments
2. Determine if the patient wishes to pay at discharge or if payment may be expected upon receipt of the bill.			
3. If the patient wishes to pay at the time of discharge, instruct the patient or family to stop at the cashier's office before leaving the hospital. Notify the cashier of the patient's intent to pay and the amount to be paid.			
4. If the patient states inability to pay upon discharge or receipt of bill, explain payment options, such as the 30/60/90-day plan.			
5. If the payment plan is selected by a patient, thoroughly explain the conditions of the option selected and obtain all necessary signatures. Document the payment arrangement selection and forward the documentation to patient financial services.			
6. Patients who absolutely refuse to discuss payment options at discharge or are unsure about the choice of payment options at discharge should be advised that they are expected to communicate with the hospital concerning any outstanding balance within 30 days of discharge.			

PROCEDURE **4** CHECKLIST

SELF-PAY NEGOTIATIONS

Competency will be considered obtained when the student has successfully completed at least five self-pay negotiations. Successful completion of this procedure is determined by satisfactory performance of each step in this checklist. All steps must be performed to the satisfaction of the instructor.

	Needs practice	Satisfactory	Comments
1. If a patient is not covered by insurance, conduct an interview with the patient or family member(s) to determine appropriate resolution.			
2. For patients who demonstrate the ability to pay, request a deposit and discuss the method for payment of the balance.			

continues

	Needs practice	Satisfactory	Comments
3. If the patient demonstrates an inability to pay, screen for public assistance programs, using the financial statement form.			
4. After exhausting all private and public health care funding, screen for hospital assistance, using the Self-Pay Allowance Income Scale to determine what recommendations should be made. If the patient qualifies for partial hospital assistance, the unaffected portion of the bill should be paid according to regular account payment procedures. Document the recommendation and notify the financial analyst in patient financial services for a review of the recommendation. The patient will receive written notification from patient financial services of the outcome of the assistance recommendation. Alert the financial analyst to any patient who could be a financial risk.			

APPENDIX B
Thinning a Medical Record

Competency will be considered obtained when the student has successfully thinned at least five medical records. Successful completion of this procedure is determined by satisfactory performance of each step in this checklist. All steps must be performed to the satisfaction of the instructor.

	Needs practice	Satisfactory	Comments
1. Identifies charts that need to be thinned.			
2. Pulls out only medication sheets and nurses' notes, leaving one day of each in the chart.			
3. Takes medication sheets and nurses' notes and assembles them in reverse chronological order.			
4. Places the thinned portion in a labeled folder in the designated area of the health unit coordinator's station.			
5. Adds back the thinned portions to the medical record upon the patient's discharge and before sending records to central medical records department.			
6. Identifies when the physician order sheets and progress notes are making the chart too thick and requests appropriate orders to thin these sections.			

APPENDIX C

Miscellaneous

▓▓▓ HOSPITAL POLICY AND PROCEDURE SUMMARY

The health unit coordinator is responsible for following policy and is required to review the following policies in full during clinical orientation. Policies should be used as references; they change as a result of new regulations and standards. Do not assume that you know a policy without frequent review.

- Consent to surgery or other medical procedure
- Advance directives
- Patient complaint management
- Information security
- Church notification
- Patient transfer
- Confidentiality of medical record information
- Accountability for patient medical record
- Medical record unit number
- Computer security
- Patient valuables and currency
- Preadmissions of inpatients
- Consent for release of general information
- Allowances and write-offs
- Lost & found
- Inpatient transfer and escort
- Transfer of attending physician responsibility

▓▓▓ PATIENT STATUS CATEGORIES

Inpatient Status
IR = Inpatient reservation (must exist before preadmit functions can be done)
IP = Inpatient preadmit (can be charged)
IA = Inpatient inactive (in hospital—assigned to other than an observation bed)
ID = Inpatient discharged (released from bed)
IC = Inpatient complete (has been billed)

Outpatient Status
OP = Outpatient preregistration
OT = Outpatient temporary (has potential to be admitted as either an inpatient or observation patient)
OA = Outpatient inactive (has little or no potential for being admitted as an inpatient or observation patient)
OC = Outpatient complete (has been billed)

INDEX